THE EDGE OF TEACHING

DISCOVER YOUR STRENGTHS
HONE YOUR SKILLS
MASTER YOUR CLASSROOM

ERIC KRUGER

The Edge of Teaching
Copyright © 2022 by Eric Kruger

All rights reserved. No part of this book may be reproduced or transmitted in any form or by any means without written permission from the author.

ISBN 979-8-9866840-0-0 Softcover
ISBN 979-8-9866840-1-7 MOBI
ISBN 979-8-9866840-2-4 ePub

Printed in USA by 48HrBooks (www.48HrBooks.com)

DEDICATION

This book is for the real ones.

To all of my colleagues over the years who looked in the mirror when there were so many other things/people to blame, who refused to give up on believing in the best for their classrooms while their buildings were culturally (and sometimes literally) falling apart, who stepped into the breach (despite being already swamped) when a coworker quit at the worst time, and who inspired me so many times with your own unique methods for success. You are the unsung heroes who have made a difference year after year when you could have done so many other things. There are so few of you and you know who you are.

This book is also for the ultimate ops manager, my beautiful wife Brittany, without whose encouragement and support this book would never have been completed. Everyone should be as lucky as I am, to have someone who loves me for who I am while still pushing me to achieve my next-level dreams!

TABLE OF CONTENTS

Preface 7
Introduction 11
Why Are You a Teacher? 15
Do You Like Kids? 17
Kids "Today" 23
Where It Starts 25
From Passion Comes Strength 31
Be the Master 41
Have a Plan 47
Manage Yourself and Your Stress 57
Love Ain't Enough 61
The Natural Laws 67
Structure and Procedure 73
Instruction for All 77
Grading 83
Relationships and "Respect" 87
Free-Floating Practical Advice 93
Conclusion 103

PREFACE

Welcome to The Edge of Teaching! My name is Eric Kruger and I'm in my fourteenth year of being an educator. While I don't think I've earned 'godfather' status yet, I like to think of myself as an 'older brother' in the business. I've been around the block: teaching Reading, Writing, or Social Studies in three major urban districts, one rural district, and in all grades from 6th-12th. It's been a wild, rewarding, and intense journey. I've learned a lot from a few good mentors and a great many mistakes. My students have come from a wide range of cultural backgrounds, but there are three things most of them have in common: the challenges of a high-poverty life, significant academic skill deficits at the start of the school year, and significant academic skill successes by the end of it.

I believe in measurable results, so here are some I'd like to share with you:

In 2011-2012 I taught 6th and 8th grade Reading at Will Rogers Junior High School in the Tulsa Public School District, Oklahoma. My 180+ students *averaged* over 2 years of reading comprehension growth in one year, as measured by our testing software. Twenty-two of my 8th graders who had failed their 7th grade English Language Arts standardized state assessment passed or earned an advanced score on their 8th grade state assessment.

I spent the next five years in Texas public school, teaching at the KIPP Austin Academy of Arts & Letters. In Texas, all public school students take the STAAR Test (State of Texas Assessment of Academic Readiness) as a standardized way to measure their academic achievement over the course of the year in certain subjects. Over this time period, I taught three different subjects and was able to compare the scores my students earned with the scores of their counterparts in every Texas public school:

2012-2013 English Language Arts, 8th Grade STAAR Test Results:
97% Students Passing
35% Students Advanced
(*Statewide Average **84%** Passing, **24%** Advanced*)

2013-2014 Social Studies, 8th Grade STAAR Test Results:
86% Students Passing
39% Students Advanced
(*Statewide Average **62%** Passing, **14%** Advanced*)

2014-15 Social Studies, 8th Grade STAAR Test Results:
91% Students Passing
30% Students Advanced
(*Statewide Average **64%** Passing, **11%** Advanced*)

2015-2016 Writing, 7th Grade STAAR Test Results:
88% Students Passing
22% Students Advanced
(*Statewide Average **70%** Passing, **11%** Advanced*)

2016-2017 Social Studies, 8th Grade STAAR Test Results:
84% Students Passing
24% Students Advanced
(*Statewide Average **62%** Passing, **18%** Advanced*)

After I moved to Kansas for my growing family, I spent the next four years teaching English and then Social Studies at Mulvane High School. During this time, only my sophomore English sections were measured with a standardized state assessment, and those results were not disaggregated to specific teachers. My first year, I noticed a significant bump in the overall scores from previous years. I'd like to think I had something to do with that, but... of course I would.

At any rate, no matter what I seem to teach or where I teach it, my students perform well. And here's the thing: Although I believe these assessments are an important measure, I believe other things to be FAR MORE important! Things like engagement in classic and challenging art, authenticity in presentation, relationships and connections with kids: real care for both the things I teach and the people I educate. I have never let the thought of standardized assessments get in the way of these things. In fact, I have never done anything in my classroom geared to a standardized assessment! Not even a multiple-choice test, unless I've been specifically told to do so by an administrator.

I relate all of this information for a few reasons. First and foremost, I want you to know that I know what I'm doing and I've proven it. There is plenty of hippy-dippy, touchy-feely stuff about teaching out there. There are also plenty of fad programs for which school districts pay top dollar. When I'm confronted with this stuff, often my first mental questions are "Who wrote this? Did it work for them in real classrooms across different environments?" Far too often, the answer to these questions is either "No" or "I have no idea." You need to know that this isn't the same thing.

And yet, this little book isn't a program or a manual. It doesn't purport to give you the one "key" or "trick" to becoming successful in the classroom. There's plenty of hippy-dippy about me, man, even though I'm a shaven-headed jock and a warrior at heart. I wrote this as a kind of letter to my younger self, as a set of pro-tips and a blueprint for realizing that the REAL key or trick was ME, and that the sooner I mastered a set of simple leadership basics and tailored my instruction to my particular strengths as a person, the better off my teaching was going to be.

That sounds simple, but in over a decade of teaching, no professional development experience I had offered it. Maybe you are a teacher early in your career, or maybe you're a veteran who might just be seeking a different angle on your own approach. Either way, my hope is to provide a short and hard-hitting set of thoughts upon which you can reflect and then execute.

Yours in the long, arduous path of leadership and instruction,

Eric

INTRODUCTION

There are many teaching books out there; what's the point of another one? There's so much available in the form of "proven" studies, approaches, and ideas for how to be a better educator, it's enough to make anyone's head spin. We're all trying to acquire the best tools to be good at our job, and so many well-meaning folks have ones to offer, but it's hard to know where to begin. I feel like I've got an important starting point. While I do want to talk about the tools to be a better teacher, first I want to talk about YOU.

You are what drives all of this. When the bell rings and the kids look up, they're looking at a human being, not a system. There are strategies, procedures, best practices, and planning cycles we can master. "X" factor, however, (the human factor of who you are and how you are as a leader of people) is an underrated part of teaching with impact. I have been to many professional development sessions and been handed almost as many books on how to improve my teaching. Too many of those sessions are the fruits of fad education thinking or are programs designed by bureaucrats who don't teach. While other sessions might feel relevant or applicable, they assume your classroom management and culture are already running smoothly. How do we cut through this fringe stuff to the basics? How do we move from the ephemeral minors on the edges to the major EDGE: you, the forged instrument, skills finely honed to sharpness, a unique combination of art and science?

This is where I feel like I've got something to say. The vast majority of my teaching career has been spent in some of the most challenging educational environments. As a Teach For America recruit, I cut my teeth in a training crash course in Harlem, NYC. It was 80-100 hour work-weeks until an abrupt transfer to my first full school year in north Tulsa, Oklahoma, nationally prominent for its inability to keep teachers in classrooms. After three years, I moved to Austin, Texas and joined the KIPP Charter network, a group of schools united behind the idea of doing whatever it takes to help students from depressed or underserved environments catch up and acquire college-ready skills. After five years at KIPP, I spent a few years in small town Kansas before returning at last to a large urban school district in Wichita.

In each of these places, I (eventually) found happiness, connection, and measurable success. While I picked up some great tools along the way from some very dynamic leaders, I knew many other educators who tried and failed to make use of those tools. I also tried and failed to use skills some of my colleagues were implementing with great success. Beyond the basic teacher moves and procedures that everyone needs to learn, there is no cookie-cutter way to a powerful and meaningful career in the classroom– to changing the lives of kids. If there were, all of these fad programs and approaches would go away, and we'd all be getting a lot out of our professional development. America would no longer be watching its educational performance metrics drop while education costs rise higher than ever.

The tools that work for me are the ones that play to my strengths as a person or at least marginalize my weaknesses. Refined over time, they continue to do both more efficiently. I actively had to seek these out over years of frustration and failure. It took a while before I realized I was even 'allowed' to do this. I was like everybody else, looking for those Holy Grail skills that All Successful Teachers acquire. I didn't realize that the real Holy Grail was within myself: my own unique passion and drive as a human being and lifelong learner, modeled for students authentically. The acquired basic teaching skills in lesson planning and managing kids were an important part of the process, but they had to flow from me.

Every time I took a step closer to that truth, I took a step forward in my career. Every time I tried to plug and play someone else's ideas with no clear connection to who I was, it fell flat. I hope that by writing this, I can distill years of reflection on that process into something that will be useful to teachers right now, or at least get them to start asking the right questions of themselves in this incredible profession.

Because I believe that so many of us can be *that* transformative teacher to a great number of our students. We can be the person that the most optimistic part of us imagined we would be when our training started. We just need to realize that the key to student engagement doesn't come from a book, course, or piece of technology. It comes from us.

I hope this book helps.

WHY ARE YOU A TEACHER?

Why are you doing this? Really.

Do you like kids? That might seem like an easy question, but I don't think it is. A lot of people claim to like kids and what they very often mean is that they like a very specific side of the kids they've seen from time to time. They like kids when they're being sweet, well-behaved, and independent-minded in a totally non-threatening way. Spoiler alert: without a lot of well-thought-through classroom management strategies and engaging lessons, this will *never* be your daily classroom (the kids you will see every single day for seven hours per day), not even in an "easy" school. It *will* be 100% your responsibility to make it right. A school year (or career) can be a very long ride if you're not psychologically prepared for that situation. Speaking of which...

How long do you plan on doing this? Is this temporary because you thought you'd teach until you got the job you truly wanted? Are you settling on this profession because you *can't* get the job you truly wanted? Do you think this will be easier? Are you one of those people who is using this experience as a resume-booster for law school or other grad school? Or one of those people who just want to move up the ladder into school administration as quickly as possible? If the answer to any of these questions is 'yes,' don't expect to get a lot out of the process. Don't expect your students to get a lot out of it, either.

I'm not knocking having other ambitions in life or saying that it's impossible to make an impact in a couple of years, but it's pretty hard to do it if you're psychologically one foot out the door before you start. Even if the commitment is short-term, I entreat you to make it a *commitment.* Treat it like the long and winding path it is, with ups and downs and a lot of required self-evaluation, and don't expect a lot of reward in a short time.

Because this great profession is truly a craft– it's an art and a science. The excellent teachers I've seen combine uniquely human, unpredictable social electricity with the aspects of a well-designed and well-oiled machine. It's a tough thing to pull off. You need to slowly master the human rhythms of leadership: the characteristics of your student age group, the times of day your classes occur, the different levels of readiness for the comprehension level of what you're teaching, how to plan for your subject area, the parts of your own personality that facilitate the engagement of your kids and need maximizing vs. the parts that don't and that need minimizing or refinement. At the same time, there are basic, almost mechanical moves and processes that need to be mastered and executed with total consistency: procedures, transitions, expectations, grading, academic behaviors. These things need to be installed, clearly explained, and work as close to 100 percent in the same way for all students, fairly and automatically, all the time.

Some leaders are born, for sure, but very few are going to just step in and be good at this. Nearly all of us will struggle with most of it in the beginning. Most of us will struggle with *some* of it forever. During those struggles, given how much is expected of us, it can be *very* easy to turn away from self-evaluation, which is hard, and start pointing fingers, which is easy. Whether it's the home lives/support/lack thereof for our students, the expectations/support/lack thereof from our school administrators and colleagues, or the general state of the education system, it's a seductively convenient (and often justifiable) excuse to blame someone else rather than continue to scrutinize our own practice. Somewhat ironically, the easiest people of all to blame are the hundred-odd ones we have to see every day in this process: the kids themselves. Which brings me back to my first question...

DO YOU LIKE KIDS?

Kids are a pain in the ass. Every age group has its thing: the crazy, energetic little kids, the sweet-but squirrelly grade schoolers, the sullen, hormone-addled large children of later middle school, the apathetic, "too cool" or angry high schoolers. We all know the types. If we're coming into a really tough school district, many of us hear the horror stories long beforehand.

Some teachers think: "No problem. I'll just train my students to behave the way they need to. I've heard stuff about some kids giving teachers a hard time, but I'm not gonna put up with that." Others say "My students will see how much I care about them and work hard for them. Love will win them over."

Beware...

Don't get me wrong: my passion for students and the individual connections I build with them (through genuine *love* for kids) are at the very center of every interaction I have in the classroom. I also don't play. I have very specific expectations in place to make sure my class flows the way I want it, and very clear procedures for what happens when it doesn't. But that takes time to develop. During and even after that time, kids are going to be kids and act out. There are very good reasons for this in every student age group. For teenagers especially, it's developmentally appropriate– they want to challenge their elders and the assumptions they've had. They question authority, and you're an authority figure, totally outside of any family (and sometimes even cultural) context for them.

If you don't *really* like kids, this is when the trouble is going to start in earnest. With how much thought and work we put into our lessons, assessments, and other plans, it can be very hard not to take it personally when the students don't play along. It's especially hard not to take it personally when you are the *person* experiencing the failure of your work, in real time, in front of a live studio audience, so to speak, and the student behavior is the visible symptom of the problem. It's hard not to say:

*Why are these **bad** kids messing with today's lesson and screwing up the learning process?*

But the truth is, there are very few truly bad kids. There are plenty of boring lesson plans, lots of poorly-conceived activities that don't work in execution, loads of unrealistic and inconsistently implemented classroom management procedures, in short: a lot of ways to manifest bad ***teaching***. And that's to be expected. Teaching is a very difficult craft to master. But in the heat and embarrassment of our stumbling and mistakes, and the annoyance at the seemingly wasted hours on plans that didn't work, what becomes far easier than the process of fixing bad teaching is to blame the students.

And that is the wrong path to go down, folks. It's a festering sore. What begins as resentment of a small group of kids on certain days becomes a general resentment of those kids before each day even begins, then general resentment of being in the classroom, and, finally, resentment of children in particular. I've seen it happen in my career many times already. Depending on the psychological makeup of the teacher, it can take a few months or a few years. However long it takes, it ruins everything.

Because the kids know when you don't like them, no matter what you might say to the contrary. Students have excellent emotional bullshit radars when it comes to us. No matter how much exemplary student work we put on our walls, cheery colors we use for decoration, or feel-good platitude posters we put up about how much we believe in them, if we resent them, they know.

And that sucks. I believe kids are good. I see it in the completely open, innocent smiles of my two young sons, and I've seen it in the faces, body language, and actions of students thousands of times. They are born excited about life and actively seek the Way/the Truth/whatever you'd like to call it. They are open-minded and very impressionable. Science tells us that how they experience life in their first seven years are key, but I know from experience that the molding and the shaping doesn't stop there. It's a beautiful and terrible thing about them: the power those few years of their lives has to frame and determine their remaining decades.

Whatever their experience, they have undergone much molding and shaping by the time they reach us, especially so the older they get. Mass culture, present adults (both major and minor influences), *absent* adults, the peer group with whom they are placed, and the food they eat all have an effect. The things they miss are as important as the active influences. *Do no harm* may be a solid first principle for the medical field, but it doesn't work for leading kids, who need active positive input. Without it, they fill the void with almost anything, bad or good... or just have a void, which can be even worse.

The truth is that we can be that active positive input *and it can make a difference.* I think a lot of people get kids confused with the screwed up adults they know. Many of those adults are totally defeated. It's not that there's no good left in them; it's that the good is so buried under a mountain of long-term accumulated bad decisions, deluded justifications, and bitter psychological habits, that it has little-to-no chance to ever see the light again in a meaningful way. Our students may be carrying a *lot*, but that mountain hasn't had the decades to build up yet. We're lucky. We've still got a chance to change something, no matter how small, and to remind them of the good that we see in them and what they can do with it.

That's really so much of what this job is about for me: to *always* see and to believe in that good, no matter what stupid decisions (out of habit or experimentation) my students happen to make. I don't mean that in the hippy-dippy poster platitude way. When my students lie, cheat, or bully people, I don't give them some empty words about how they're beautiful people with good hearts. That's bullshit– and the student knows more than anyone. I see far too many teachers making *zero* real, personalized connections with students, and then suddenly trying to show up in disaster time with some Hallmark card positive reinforcement.

Real connection– real *love* for kids is to still be ready, vulnerable, and paying attention when they actually *do* something good, something that took effort and decision to carry out– no matter how many things they do/don't do normally that we happen to dislike. To know whether or not that student likes public or private praise, to know what your normal 'vibe' is with that student, and when to disrupt it versus when to just go with it, and to make clear, one way or another, that you saw the good thing, you truly noticed it for what it was, and you *took it in* and thought to yourself: "good job."

Our students, who are individuals still seeking that right *Way* no matter how much time they might spend on their phones, are looking for that acknowledgement. When we get resentful, or too stressed out by classroom management, or too discouraged at the failure of our carefully-laid plans, we miss those opportunities. We miss out on "I love kids" and "I believe in kids" being anything more than empty words.

For example, I had a student who had repeatedly cheated on assignments. Each time, I had the conversation about what that meant and why the assignment was going to receive a zero. It was far from her only exhibition of sneaky behavior. She knew all of these things, but she was still mad. A couple of days later, when I dropped by her discussion group, (seats in my class are grouped for discussion and interaction) she went out of her way to be rude to me in front of her group-mates, completely unprovoked. From where I was in my "reasonable" perception of how the world is supposed to work, it really pissed me off. Totally out of line. I bit back my rising rage and dealt with the issue according to my standard fashion, on a low level, and as one-to-one as it could get. Nothing extra.

It stung. I could feel myself shying away from that group in the following days, not wanting a repeat of the anger or even the awkwardness. But I forced myself to follow through with my normal rounds anyway, like nothing happened, still investigating the level of engagement and understanding of the material I had taught them. I pointed things out, asked questions, and commented on work like nothing had happened. Then, about a week after the incident, I noticed the student put together a really good conclusion of her own in the space where the students record their discussion question answers. It was backed by evidence that I could see none of her group peers had thought to use. This seemed low-stakes, because I don't have the kids turn in their discussion answers, but I casually paused and quietly let the rest of them know that she had an angle on the discussion question that none of them had, because she had thought of evidence they hadn't taken into account. Then I looked her right in the face and said, like it was no big deal: "really good job."

This might sound absurd, but this was a game-changing moment in the relationship I had with this student. It was a tiny, seemingly inconsequential, but *100 percent authentic* and personalized way for me to show this kid that I still believed in her, was still watching, and ready to see the best she had. If I had waited for her to get an A on some major essay, I would have been waiting the rest of the year. If I had gone out of my way to manufacture a way to praise her, it would have rung hollow at best, or sent the wrong message completely (that I needed to make things *right* after making her mad) at worst. If I had taken the easy route, which was to avoid the student and the awkwardness completely, I would have reinforced the idea some children want to believe: that teachers only care when rules get broken. I waited for the right time, carefully investing small amounts of observation on Little Miss Attitude Sneaky. And it made a difference.

Months later, this student was still getting that pencil right to paper on discussion questions. With her newly-reinforced belief that her original thoughts and critical eye could be put up against the history material, over time, her essays improved. I continued to positively reinforce, one small authentic success after another. Her average gradually rose from a 39 to a 75. More importantly, her critical thinking skills were honed. All because of that one interaction? No. Because I like kids enough, and believe in their critical thinking ability enough, that continued observation and investment, although sometimes painful and annoying, allowed me to see the opportunity for a shift when it came.

If you *truly* like kids, times like these are when it matters. Be ready.

KIDS "TODAY"

I know what you might be thinking.

So that's <u>one kid.</u> Do you really notice every little thing every kid does when you assign them something? (Sort of– more on that later) *I've got 25 other kids in class! And a lesson to teach. And a whole lot of those kids are more than willing to be distracted by anything! These kids today, with the smartphones, and the clothes, and the hormonal drama, and the 10 second attention spans! It ain't like the good old days, with those 25 students in perfect rows, with perfect posture, like in the old pictures, when you got paddled for speaking out of turn!* **These** *kids need everything handed to 'em and don't want to learn!!*

So I just rattled off a silly caricature, but I can't tell you how many times per year I hear refrains that sound an awful lot like parts of this one. And I get it, to a degree. Our culture has certainly never been more easily distracted than it is right now, and phone technology is one big symptom. The internet and modern diets exacerbate loads of other problems, but if you're going to blame them, you're lying to yourself.

I was in one of the final groups of American kids to grow up without the internet. When I graduated high school in 1997, a fraction of my classmates had steady access to it, but it had not yet become the cultural force it would be later. Cell phones were for the elite only. I didn't know a single person among the 800-plus people with whom I attended school who owned one. And you know what? We had plenty of behavior issues, plenty of bad grades, and plenty of classrooms where a whole lot of learning was *not* happening– where distracted, disaffected students went about distracting other students.

We *did* have sugar, fast food, television with its dumbed-down mass culture, and a lot of the other crap people point to as the stuff that's ruining kids. It's a fair point. I hate all of those things. But you know what we also had? Plenty of kids who learned plenty of stuff, and a few classrooms where everybody got to the end of the year and said something like– "Great class. I learned a lot in that class. I thought I wasn't going to like it, but I did." After years spent in a few vastly different education environments, I can tell you I notice the same thing today.

And you might as well forget those old black and white pictures of perfect classrooms. I wonder how perfect some of them were outside of the posed photos. This is just one anecdotal example, but I chuckle sometimes when I've read *To Kill a Mockingbird* with students– the descriptions of the hapless little schoolhouse teacher unable to handle her rowdy grade school students– in early twentieth century, strait-laced, rural Alabama. Kids of the past, present, and future could take over a classroom with foolishness or destroy it with apathy. They could also learn more (while having fun) than they ever imagined, despite their background or their preconceptions. Don't be one of those people that falls into that "old man on the front porch" rut of blaming today's culture and kids for a bad classroom. There are other things, completely under your control, that play a huge role in determining whether or not students are engaged in what you have to teach.

Like *you.*

WHERE IT STARTS

For a moment, forget all that stuff about making engaging and relevant lessons. We'll get to that later. Are *you* engaging and relevant?

I think it's an underrated question. Schools (and plenty of other places) have posters, placards, and syllabi filled with corny platitudes galore: *follow your heart, believe in yourself, live a full life, be yourself.* Do *you* live by those words? Can the kids see it? *Be the change you want to see in the world*. We say this stuff to kids and more often than not it comes off like useless hot air, because we don't provide any kind of example.

We will always have students that come into our classes fired up and ready because they already love our subject/had a teacher that helped them appreciate the subject. But for everyone else, the learning process in your class is going to involve getting out of their comfort zone, somewhat, if it's going to be successful. It's going to involve taking a risk with mental energy. Learning new skills and being vulnerable to new passions is an uncomfortable process most of the time. It's a whole lot easier to do if the teacher is already a living example of how to do it well.

It's the same with 'being yourself.' The ironically overarching message the average school building sends during class time is to *not* be yourself. Everyone must conform to a standard set of behaviors and procedures, so that the required objectives can be achieved. I'm not knocking that: I think it's necessary to some extent within the confines of what we've got to do in school. A building full of 500+ young people must learn a boatload of skills, whether they like it or not, after all.

That makes it even more incumbent upon us to let ourselves– our best and true selves– shine through within the parameters of a successful learning environment. This is hard for a lot of people to do. Look around many classrooms, and you'll see a lot of standard classroom posters, colors, maybe a posed family or baby picture or two. I think: where is the unique person here? What are the interests they explore? What do they do with the people they love? What stimulates their mind? What are their other passions?

Well, that's none of the students' business. I'm here to teach and they're here to learn. This is like their first real job.

While this sentiment is applicable in specific and individual cases, I've got an issue with it as a teaching philosophy. Kids *are* with us to learn, and we *are* here to teach– but not just our subject area. Whether we like it or not, the children who spend seven hours per day in our buildings are learning a whole lot from us about how to be a person. What we teach them (consciously or unconsciously, verbally or nonverbally) can make quite an impact.

There is no more powerful leadership than by example. We all know it's true, but we have a hard time living it. Are you boring? Not your subject– *you*. If yes, why? If no, does your classroom reflect that? Does your classroom reflect *you*?

I can remember when I first began to truly grasp this– around year three of my teaching career. Up to that point, my classroom had been comically spartan. I couldn't put up the standard posters and frills and sayings. I consider myself a pretty authentic person and I hate 'cookie cutter.' But I didn't know what else should go up there, either. So my classroom walls were about as depressing and stripped as possible. But I had noticed that my students seemed to respond well to me as a person, especially the stuff I wore on my sleeve that wasn't stuff they were used to seeing in a teacher.

I like adventure, heavy music, history, guerrilla movements, strength sports, intense stories, good cooking, and good conversation. I especially like stuff that combines anything on that list. My students would laugh when these things would become apparent: sometimes **at** me, because they thought it was ridiculous, sometimes out of sheer bemusement, because they weren't used to it. Many other times, they'd laugh or smile in appreciation, either because they connected with that part of me, or (I think) because they appreciated that I'd let them see that part of me, whether they were going to connect with it or not. It takes vulnerability to do that.

I would work it in here and there. When explaining analogies or metaphors, I would use a personal example from those unusual parts of myself. I started posting pictures. I would have my cooked lunch sitting there ready to go, or the dish would be out after I was done with it, filling the classroom with the smell of the food. Whatever book I was reading would be right on my desk. The students could see that I remained an avid strength athlete, because I made sure to keep my training up. I would get animated and nerdy when asked about any of my weird interests, even in front of a whole classroom.

I didn't awkwardly force it on the kids and I didn't make a big deal out of it, but it stood out: Mr. Kruger was a *character*. As time went by, I noticed this (and its benefits in connecting with students) more and more; by year three my whole classroom began to reflect it. I spent time over the summer painting copies of my favorite rebel, guerrilla, and underground art that my limited talents could manage. I printed some of my favorite heavy music lyrics right along with my favorite poems from the likes of Blake and Coleridge. I blared death metal during detention. I stapled the poor-quality pictures of my road trips (taken with a cheap camera) to the wall. I drew a to-scale M-79 grenade launcher in Sharpie marker as a logo underneath my name in giant impact-font letters. My assistant principal thought I was completely nuts.

And the kids ate it right up. Whatever else I was doing, I was 100 percent **being myself** every day. The students believed in the sincerity of every word I said and every action I undertook. They were also unquestionably watching me live life and learn while I was doing it. It's difficult to understate how important these things are for everything we try to accomplish in our classrooms. "Love of learning" and "be yourself" might sound like the corny goal phrases you hear at big professional development meetings twice per year, but why not model them? Not talk about them: actually model them. It's scary, but as long as it's authentic, your students will respect it.

We all have stuff that deeply interests us. Follow that stuff and use your classroom walls to show it off. If there's a learning process to it (even better), make mistakes, get better at it, and joyfully present the evidence. It can be anything– flowers, model planes, fishing, metalwork, amateur carpentry, sourdough bread: who knows? The possibilities are endless. The more niche it is, the better. It makes you a real and unique person.

There's a school of thought that says we need to try to understand and connect with what the **kids** think is cool. I disagree with that. First of all, while there are a few of us who might be able to pull it off (because the connection is a **real** and **adult** one), for most of us, it's going to look like a painfully obvious attempt to ingratiate ourselves. That's rarely a good start with any relationship, let alone one with kids. If you genuinely enjoy scrolling social media looking for topical memes or viral sensations and can make a real connection from that to your teaching material, ok. If it's already **you**.

If that's not you, and you are just trying to find a way to be a cool adult, beware: once it becomes apparent to the kids that being cool matters to you, you're in trouble. And they can smell it a mile away. Our students are surrounded all day by hundreds of peers who are insecure and desperate for acceptance. Don't be another one of those people. Don't even look like one for a second. It will cheapen everything you are trying to bring to the table.

Besides, our job is not to be accepted by them, but to lead them– to higher knowledge, to essential ways of thinking, to important skills, to something **better** that adulthood is supposed to bring. It's good to be above the stuff the kids think is hilarious or relevant. Not above it in an angry, arrogant, or bitter way– just aware with the years of experience we have that **true relevance** cuts deeply enough that it doesn't need the help of the social norms and ideas of the teenage world.

At different times during my adulthood, I decided to learn the best way to brew coffee, learn how to smoke meat the old fashioned way, drive across the West to California, and to compete in a Highland Games. I didn't do any of these things to look cool. I did those things because the process in each one revealed something awesome about life. The way in which those experiences did that for me is partly shown in who I am, but can be shown further in plain words to any person who listens. If we can be people who clearly live life to our unique specifications, learn through the process, and understand what's awesome about it, we are being the kind of leader our students need in a way that transcends what's trendy or "relevant."

More importantly, from that position of authentic leadership, it's a short step to revealing what's awesome and truly relevant about the process of the subject we teach– not just to students in school, but to anyone.

FROM PASSION COMES STRENGTH

It's a good thing my first subject (English) is awesome, because every other aspect of the start of my teaching career was inauspicious at best. As a thirty year old waitlisted Teach For America applicant, I had about three and a half weeks between my admission and when I shipped out for our training Institute in New York City. I hadn't been in front of a class in three years, and that was as a Teaching Assistant at the University of Texas where I was a graduate student. I began Institute with very little preparation.

Institute is a controversial teacher training program. Teach For America selects people with college degrees who are willing to accept a two year commitment to teach in "high-need" areas of the country. These people have typically little to no education in the craft of teaching and will do the bulk of their learning on the job. Before they start in the fall of their first teaching year, however, they receive a six week training course during the summer in a "high need" district while they simultaneously teach under constant professional supervision.

What this amounted to (in my case) was six weeks of 90-100 hours of work, teaching, planning, meeting, reflecting, and learning in professional classes. It took place in Harlem, New York City, while our cohort of new teachers stayed together in double and triple dorm rooms on St. John's University campus, far up in Queens (45 minutes on trains or at least an hour by bus away from our teaching site). While I found this experience both incredibly challenging and vitally useful, for the purposes of this story, my preparation for my first classroom was a six-week crash course that utterly exhausted me. I relocated my life to my two-year assignment in Tulsa, Oklahoma two days after its completion. I was then teaching my first class less than two weeks later. At a time when I really needed a few days off, I was on my own with students for the very first time and trying to learn on the job!

In addition to this, my school was failing (it was closed at the end of my second year), its neighborhood in Tulsa had a notoriously high murder and crime rate, half of the teaching staff were Teach For America first-year corps members like me (read: didn't know the first thing about teaching), and kids were in and out of my school all the time as their parents or guardians were on the move. I finished year one with one third of the students who started the year with me. This was hardly a recipe for success.

Hell, I even **looked** pretty bad. I was broke and still wearing old 'nice clothes' that needed to be replaced. They weren't going to be replaced any time soon: Oklahoma teacher pay is pathetic. I made more money in tips at my car wash job in New Jersey than I made as a full-time teacher with a master's degree in Tulsa. As a very difficult two years dragged on, bills and stress mounted, and I got less and less consistent about washing or ironing those old clothes. My outward classroom appearance was barely acceptable. Combined with everything else, my teaching experience should have been an unmitigated disaster. Except it wasn't.

The start was very rough, don't get me wrong. I did a whole bunch of culture building stuff that was a hard sell along with some foundational lessons and goal-setting, just like TFA suggested, only for the makeup of my classes to alter drastically on week 3. "After about two weeks we really figure out the schedule" was what I was told. About one third of my students then had no idea about anything I'd done for the first two weeks (not that I'd executed those two weeks particularly well). I was trying to plan and teach the way I thought TFA would want, based on my Institute experience: clear objectives, clear lesson steps, and measurable assessments. Those are actually all really important, but in the absence of any real idea of how to do things, I was totally focused on the mechanics of the lesson cycle, rather than what would make lessons interesting. It was boring, to say the least.

To make matters worse, the vast majority of my students were years behind in reading comprehension and writing skills. Most were quite incapable of independently reading the on-grade-level material we were issued. These students certainly weren't going to be exercising the critical thinking necessary to practice the skills they were expected to learn in the lessons. Students were not only bored; they were frustrated with the genuine difficulty of what they were being asked to do. These two things fed into each other and formed a negative feedback loop: the more frustrated they were, the less inclined they were to invest in the boring procedural nature of my instruction. This was true for me as well: the harder I worked on planning good lessons, the less I got out of it, which made me less inclined to keep working so hard, especially when teaching every day at my struggling school was psychologically exhausting in the first place. By late October, I was just hanging on and winging it every day. Not good.

Out of desperation, I finally began to ask myself: "What am I *good* at?" TFA assigned a Program Director to each one of us (program director was one of TFA's many shifting administrative titles for 'person who is supposed to support you and develop you as a teacher.' I know the professional title has changed a couple of times since). My PD, Jay, had been by a couple of times and mentioned that he thought my class was the most engaged when I was reading to them, and they were following along. I sucked at just about everything else, so I threw away everything else I was repeatedly failing to do and took this as a starting point. It made sense: while I was a strength athlete and wrestler, in high school and college I had always enjoyed theater and performance. If I was passionate about something, I could have stage presence.

So I picked out a couple of novellas I really liked. I re-skimmed them and thought about how to fashion reading comprehension exercises around their plots: when and how to ask the right questions. I drew up really simple lessons on the basics of how to think about stories (plot structure, figurative language, inferences, etc.) that would take a short period of time, then have practice through reading aloud. When I could manage it, I had little multiple choice quizzes and/or questions for the kids to answer, so I could see how well they were comprehending things.

The difference was almost immediate. Some TFA support folks suggested I make sure the kids had the books in front of them, following along with eyes or a pencil. This was a good little tweak: it gave me a nonverbal, physical cue for who was along for the ride and who was not, and lent itself to a very simple correction ("eyes on the book" or even something nonverbal). I had to make plenty of those corrections, but the bulk of the class was now at least partly engaged, every day. Improvement! I laugh now, but it's not really a laughing matter: these small steps mean a lot and they give you a base upon which you can build. Whatever my kids thought of English class, they were definitely enjoying and learning more from my reading out loud.

I think modeling my passion for the subject was the difference. Given the aforementioned circumstances, I don't know what else possibly could have been. I had a classroom nearly three quarters full of students who were in agreement that they hated reading. I told them I loved to read, but that only elicited bemused shakes of the head. I had to show them *why* I loved reading and *how* to love reading. Truly good stories provide some kind of insight into the human condition: through humor, tragedy, conflict, or something else unique to our species with which any human can at least somewhat connect. I delight in the process of that happening, and once I'd tossed all of the things that weren't working and began from a spot of showing kids how I delighted in the development of stories and their characters, I started to gain traction.

I reflected on how I processed stories as I read them, following the narrative and the clues an author would leave: about a character's development, building anticipation for a future event, or just skilled use of figurative language in a way that created a powerful image or an ambiguous meaning. When I previewed the text I was reading aloud for the next few days, I would find those spots and depending on the standards that needed taught that week, use those places to stop during the reading and ask questions about those situations out loud. My short lessons would be primed to work with the text in this fashion, rather than text picked to fit lessons or objectives.

My penchant for performance was a big help. I inhabited the characters, altering my reading voice to fit my ideas of how certain characters were when I spoke their dialog. Even when it was clumsy or made the kids laugh, it helped to transmit the feel and meaning of what was going on to struggling students. When dealing with challenging levels of reading comprehension and critical thinking skills, anything that eliminates basic confusions without dumbing down the narrative is useful. And all along there was *my* character, Mr. Kruger the Narrator, pausing at dramatic or reflective moments saying right out loud:

"Whoa, wait a minute. Why is she doing this?"

With wait time for thinking or discussion, the multiple different 'right answers' could trickle in: some focused on connecting the character's decision with patterns in her behavior from earlier, some with anticipation of what her character might have thought the consequences might be, some with details about the current environment of the story and how they might have affected decision-making. Often, this would spark back-and-forth between my students in agreement or disagreement, and I could gently guide this discussion with further questions.

Whatever label you might want to give it, this was *reading*. If I had opened that particular day with bland definitions of the skill they needed to learn, straight from the standard, then applied practice examples without any context, I wonder if I might have turned most students off right from the start. I worked with examples from the novel, using context from the novel: the continuous story we were reading with the characters I already knew very well, which made things easier to explain and provided a greater point of human connection for the students– both with me and the humans in the story I had selected.

I think it's important to note here that I had picked novellas *I* loved. In education, we hear an awful lot about how important it is to gear your lessons towards what's culturally relevant to your students. This is certainly worth doing if you can manage it, but when our chief problem is in getting students to enjoy learning about our subject, I think it's hardly ever wrong to start from a place in which we model *true enjoyment and passion* for what we are teaching– whatever that may be. When in doubt, start with what *you* love. At the very least, it's easy to model the passion for what you are teaching, and modeling is one of the most powerful weapons we have in our arsenal as leaders of young people.

In my first three months of teaching, if I had asked my students what they wanted to read, many would have said "nothing; I hate reading." Others might have suggested the kind of low level page-turning stuff that would not have allowed me to teach critical thinking skills with any level of appropriate challenge. Fine for student independent reading maybe, but not fine for instruction. Perhaps a few would have suggested some books that might have been appropriate, but that I'd never read. Without knowing it or having read it, I could not have known its quality, much less how I would build my instruction around it.

And what if there was a text that was engaging to students AND an appropriate challenge, but I just didn't like it? I would need to first question myself: is my mind too closed? We all miss out on good things from time to time for precisely this reason. Did I give it a true chance, or did I just give it a once-over and let my prejudices do the rest? Did I feel ok about it, but not see its relevance as a text worthy of instruction? If I can't confidently answer these questions in the right way, then I need to choose a different text. Your attempt to connect with kids in a way you don't sincerely respect is going to ring hollow and undermine everything about your instruction. Once again: students can smell bullshit a mile away.

Whatever we are when we step in front of classrooms, it is vitally important that we *not* be bullshit. Young people (especially in the twenty-first century) are bombarded with bullshit all day: advertising campaigns, insincere friends, hypocritical adults, social pressures around unimportant things. The older these young people are, the more attuned and sensitive they are to the flaws in their adult counterparts and any inauthenticity they might display. Even well-meaning inauthenticity is a bad thing. It is profoundly lame: an adult so clueless and eager to please that he is floundering around with anything "the kids think is cool." What does it say about your subject that this is the level to which you must be reduced in its instruction? Let authenticity be your guide, even when it appears to be lame, and you can never be on a completely wrong path.

I got to see this personally. When I owned this approach, things often began with laughs, rolled eyes, or indifference. But as time went by, more and more of my students would shift into gear the moment we were all reading. I would stand at my doorway in between periods, and hear students of mine talking about the books we read, even using the academic language I had trained them to use in my brief lessons. More importantly, by year's end, when we conducted our measurable tests, both the state-administered kind and the reading comprehension kind, I noticed some very good news.

First, my kids did no worse, and mostly better, on the state-administered tests than their counterparts with different teachers in the same building or similar Tulsa schools. While I'll say more on the subject of state tests and how credible they are later, I found this to be encouraging. Most of those other teachers had teaching degrees and several years more experience than I had. To not be measurably worse than them in what was undoubtedly going to be the worst phase of my career felt like a win.

Second, I kept track of the group of my students with whom I had spent the entire year, and another group with whom I had spent at least a half year. Each of these sample groups made significant progress in reading comprehension as per our TFA-directed tests and the numbers were clear: the longer they had been with me, the more they had progressed. Many of them had made the 'gold standard' measure of catching up when behind in reading comprehension: making two or more years of comprehension growth in one year of instruction. That too felt like a win.

This all started with something very simple: sharing what I deeply loved in my subject area, and doing it along with my kids every day. The love rubbed off and gave the thinking skills enough grease to get started.

Then the kids were practicing the skills over and over through the stories. The learning process is so much easier when you are enjoying yourself while doing it. I bitched and complained endlessly about equations in math class when I was a high school student. Then I went home and tied my brain in knots trying to figure out the hard levels in video games—*which were really nothing more than solving equations.* Sure, they were dressed up with pictures of vampire hunters carrying whips or incarnate angels with wings and swords, but at the end of the day they were a totally rational set of problems involving rates of speed and number values in combination. They just had a fun factor that my math classes did not. I believe *every* subject can be fun when its instruction begins with the same passion shared from its true nerds.

After all, if *we're* not vocally sharing our joy in the process, or worse, if we don't have **any** joy in the process, how can we expect the students to be engaged in it? I see well-meaning teachers trying to be "realistic" with students and colleagues by 'admitting' that (to use just a few possible examples):

    History is dry.
    Math is boring.
    Science is confusing.
    English is not always relevant to real life.
    NO!

This is like beginning a chess game with a concession of total strategic defeat. We cannot believe this. We must not utter it. Whatever our curriculum is and however corrupted its presentation has become through decades of bloated school administrative bureaucracy, it is deeply connected to something vitally important in human experience and human progress. Something other than sheer boredom or desire for money (ha!) made you want to share this with rooms full of young people. Some part of you remembers being young and discovering, in no matter how small a way, that deep and vital connection.

What was that? Start there and build everything, brick by brick, from that foundation of passion. I believe it to be a powerful tool in getting your students engaged and keeping you refreshed and invested. In my eighth grade English class, there were no programs, no computers, no phones, *definitely* no worksheets, and (after the first few weeks) not even a textbook. I'm not saying this was ideal or that this is all there is to great teaching– if I could go back to those first two years now, I'd do several things very differently. But it is a foundation upon which anyone can build, and the better you know your subject area, the stronger that foundation will be. Speaking of which…

BE THE MASTER

I have written a lot so far about what to bring with you before you even step into a classroom and attempt to execute units and lessons. In addition to true belief in kids and true passion for your subject, I would like to add one more seemingly obvious thing: mastery of your content.

There's a reason the *true master*– the elderly Kung Fu immortal at the top of a mountain, the sage hermit in the desert, the silent, expert gunfighter character in the classic Western films– is an archetype that appears in stories over and over. We don't know how long it took the Master to acquire all the knowledge necessary or what the Master had to do to get it. We do know that the Master is a living embodiment of an art or mode of thinking, and if we were to be a student to that Master, it would be possible to learn *everything* about it.

This need not be only for highfalutin concepts. I can remember my summer job from my late teens, working as a laborer for a New Jersey builder. One of our projects involved the construction of a new wing on an old church. One morning, as we worked high up, I got to watch a small crew of guys come and put in the new wood flooring on the wide, open area of the first floor. It was incredible. In case you aren't familiar: to the inexperienced, putting in hardwood floors sucks. There are so many ways to make tiny mistakes that screw up everything. These guys just blew right through it: you could see the years of deep practice and correction in every small movement of their backs, hands, wrists, even fingers. Moving quickly! The subtlety combined with speed was one of the more impressive physical feats I've ever seen in my life. This job would have taken me all week and they had it finished by lunch. As silly as it might sound, they were obvious Masters and there was something mystical about being in the same room with them and recognizing that fact.

While I had (and have) absolutely no interest in a career laying flooring, something then (and even still) in watching that performance made me interested in knowing the art a lot better. In a culture that grows more shallow, distraction-heavy, and deconstructed with every passing decade, there is an inner light that shines ever more brightly in one that has taken the time and the energy to *really know* something. I wish our leaders in education put more of a premium on this kind of approach to what we teach.

As educators, we get exposed to many hours of professional development per year. Nearly all of it during the course of my career has been focused on things that have nothing to do with increasing (or engaging with) my depth of knowledge in what I actually teach. There are sessions on using technology, increasing student engagement, planning assessments, the emotional health of students, etc. These are all worthy topics for professional development, but I'd love to see some of that time devoted to extra learning and discussion of content matter: A curriculum-specific book club for English teachers, a district-wide session on the Vietnam War for U.S. history teachers, etc. I'd like to see time to learn more from books and other experts in the subject we love.

Depth is so important, especially at the highest levels of our subject. If we are going to unlock those levels for kids, we have to be better– to be able to confidently show them the relevance and fun in the complexity of what we're asking them to master. If we are intimidated by it or 'too cool' for it (very often the same thing), it's going to be hard to achieve anything special. I'll dive into an example here specifically from my field, but try if you can to relate it to something excellent in your own field. I want to talk about William Shakespeare.

I can't tell you how many times I've heard teachers of high school English say they "hate" Shakespeare. I have several problems with this attitude. First of all, (and related to my idea of passion as a guiding force) if you're telling your students you don't like Shakespeare while in the process of starting a three week *Romeo and Juliet* or *Macbeth* unit, you are about to waste everyone's time. Any kid not already a fan of Shakespeare is going to take your leadership cue (because that's what it is) and use it as permission to disengage at the first sign of confusion or trouble. And what a shame that would be, both for their education *and* their enjoyment.

Furthermore, *why don't you like Shakespeare?* Really. He's regarded as one of the greatest writers of all time. I assure you, it's not because the English language has a shortage of playwrights and poets who know 'fancy' words. Shakespeare was a master of language, yes– and this can be seen in every multi-layered metaphor and clever use of literary sound devices. He was also a master of real human experience and emotion, who understood how a hero can go tragically bad, or a villain can become self-reflective. His writing is complex and can be hard to penetrate, yes– like the expert level of just about anything worth doing. Greatness can't *always* be in simplicity. What's not to like?

Could it be that *you* don't really get it? That you haven't really bothered to try? First of all, that's a shame, because you're missing out, I promise. Secondly, how in the world are we supposed to guide kids to an understanding of why Shakespeare was an important writer if we ourselves don't understand? We can do better, and we should. I see far too many English teachers blowing through their Shakespeare or Transcendentalist units as quickly as possible– *even having the students read large sections of these texts independently, with no help.* If you, the teacher, can't be bothered to grapple with a true great, do you think your students can, un-aided?

Most of our students are behind, some woefully behind, in reading comprehension level. Even for the highest readers, breaking down Shakespeare can be hard. For students who are behind, you might as well be asking them to read Chinese. It's absurd. At best it's a waste of time; at worst it further ingrains the hatred of young people for some of the greatest art our cultural heritage has produced. How could they do anything *but* hate it? Attempting an expert level project when you have only beginner skills is a profoundly frustrating experience. Eagle Claw Kung Fu is not to be self-taught out of a book. You need Master Pai Mei on the mountaintop to show you the *Way*– the moves and the mode of thinking behind those moves.

This is where you come in. You might not be Pai Mei, but you can be a whole lot better than you are– and this is a time in which it's fun to get better. All of us enjoy greatness in action and truly understanding what makes it great. If we can understand why Shakespeare is great (and Shakespeare is only one example of great written art) and illuminate it for our students, we've done something important: not just for them, but for art itself and the humanities.

Great art and the appropriately-named "humanities" is a large part of what separates us from the animals. For most of human history, there wasn't any great art that survived, which was a shame. It dies without careful maintenance, preservation... and teaching. Showing kids that there are universal aspects to human experience that are beautiful, tragic, uplifting, and crushing– and that they can be uniquely expressed in a way with which we can all connect– is the incredible job of the humanities teacher.

So, if you don't like it/get it/whatever, you should learn how. I've known several English teachers who don't like the wave of anti-intellectualism hitting the mainstream, but then admit they read almost nothing but young adult novels. Come on. Who is going to model swimming in the deep end of the pool for these kids, if not you? Put down the "No Fear Shakespeare" and dive in. Take a course with a professor who is also a good teacher. When I was barely getting by on my stipend peanuts as a grad student at the University of Texas, I had a wonderful time as a Teaching Assistant for English professors. Their lectures for non-majors opened a whole new world of thinking and interpretation for me. They were connecting with the skeptics and the students who weren't interested in the subject and it taught me a lot about both the literature *and* how to make that connection. It was truly an adventure. Can't take a physical course? Explore online options or at least get a companion book that can walk you through some of this stuff. I think you'll truly discover why it's been considered great art for so long.

As a teacher of Shakespeare, Renaissance, transcendentalists, guerrillas, romantics, Vikings, memoirs, and *everything* in between, I walk into my classroom every day aware of my quest to illuminate their greatness and universality for my students. As the years have gone by, I have never stopped exploring everything I teach for my own nerdy enjoyment, but also to think and plan for how to relate that greatness and universality to students and others. Whatever the individual topic, I begin with the question for myself:

"Why is this important/awesome?"

As much as possible, I want to wade into teaching each learning objective with an answer I can speak with total conviction. I want to be fired up about that answer. If a kid gives the typical "Who cares?" or "What does this have to do with my life?" kind of verbal volley, I want to have a reply I can say while looking them right in the face. And for that reply to have nothing to do with state standards, or curriculum plans, good grades, or their need for a high school diploma to succeed.

In old Catholicism, the Pope is called the pontiff– a term (probably) coming from the old Latin word *pontifex,* with the roots *pons* (bridge) and *facere* (to make/build/do). As head of the Church, the Pope was the one with the responsibility to *build the bridge* for mankind to something deeper, more awesome, and more important than all its individuals could possibly comprehend while walking around in life, left to their own devices. In a much smaller way, that's you: building the bridge between the greatness of your subject and the individuals in your classroom who are unaware of it. Your students should be able to see that in you and perceive that if there is any Truth to your subject, you will be able and willing to help them through the hard work of crossing over to it. You may be the only chance these kids have in their lives at that bridge getting built.

Be aware of that fact. It's far more important than any new trend or program in teaching skills.

HAVE A PLAN

Teaching skills, however, are still extremely important. The first and foremost of these, in my opinion, involves a plan for exactly what your students need to learn over the course of a school year. It can be very easy for the days to start to run together and for us to lose our idea of whether our students have mastered and retained what they need to know. At the end of the day, this is the job, after all. I've met a few people who seem to think that building relationships with kids and giving a general overall effort is good enough. "They just need love and understanding!" Yes, but they also need thinking and practical skills, and that's actually what you were hired to provide.

Don't be one of those people that hides behind *great relationships with kids.* All too often that's code for being a generally popular teacher because very little is expected of the students in class. Any trade school, law school, or med school that boasted good relationships with students but failed to provide them with any concrete skills for their jobs would lose all credibility pretty quickly. The stakes might seem higher in those schools, but that's just because of the extra money spent out of pocket by individual attendees. The life stakes are much higher in grades K-12, where we are entrusted with preparing kids for the bare minimums of being a citizen and adult. If we fail to measurably bring kids to the level they need (or catch them up some when they're already behind), the lifelong implications are serious in both tangible ways (jobs and pay) and intangible ways (missing out on deep and enjoyable paths because they never get the basics).

So how do we know if we've taught what we need to teach? As most of you probably know, every state has a published list of standards for every subject in every grade level, broken down into main groups and sub-groups, sometimes even down to the smallest objectives one can cover in a single teaching day. Finding and reading these is the easy part. But how do we ultimately judge if the students *know* them? That must be the marker, after all, of whether we've done a good job.

Many states have moved aggressively towards standardized tests given late in the year as a measure of what students have learned and retained. At first glance, this has many aspects that recommend it. A team of professionals designs a test through a secret process and no teacher can view it until the testing day. By keeping test design separate from the teachers in the actual classrooms, the idea is that a rigorous, high standards assessment has a better chance: no bias, laziness, or self-justification on the part of teachers can affect the end product. Ideally, the designers can write a strict adherence to the state standards into the test, and ultimately we will be able to see if students (and by extension, teachers) measured up in the classroom.

This has been a controversial initiative, to say the least. For one thing, the further and further a student falls behind in comprehension skills, the harder and harder each year's test will be. I have had colleagues teaching Algebra 2 with students in the classroom who have barely (or not) mastered multiplication. As an eighth grade reading teacher, I was supposedly dealing with texts at the complexity of JRR Tolkien's *The Hobbit,* while about one third of my students showed up on the first day of class with reading skills just above *Hop on Pop* by Dr. Seuss. Is it the teacher's fault if these students aren't adequately prepared for their end-of-year tests in Algebra 2 or 8th Grade English?

Another large problem with standardized state test design is that it is often skewed towards certain kinds of assessment, like multiple choice questions. While multiple choice questions have their place, it can be difficult for them to represent the kind of deep, layered critical thinking we want our students to execute. When they do have a correct answer that reflects this level of thinking, if a student gets the question wrong, it can be impossible to tell what went wrong and for what reason.

I have had excellent history students who get a question wrong because they are English Language Learners and weren't familiar with many more arcane words in a primary source passage. History standard lists are often incredibly long and complicated, covering more things than could possibly be taught in-depth during a school year. I have spent an entire week on an eighth grade Civil War unit, with my students producing excellent essays tying the causes of the conflict, the events, the outcomes, and the subsequent effects of the conflict on American culture, only to have one of the three state test questions on the topic be a very specific one about Stonewall Jackson. In this instance, I hadn't spent much time on Stonewall Jackson other than his great effect on the early progress of the war. Over two thirds of my kids bombed the question. In grading the performance of the students on the Civil War skills, (and really, my performance as a Civil war teacher), one of the three grades was 33 percent. Even if performance on the other two questions was stellar, my students looked average at best, when all the data had been analyzed. Meanwhile, I knew for a fact that unit had been one of the most successful of the entire year.

 I have seen similar issues in English instruction. A state exam often features a reading passage followed by several multiple choice questions designed to test the student's recognition of the importance of the passage or ability to synthesize various required skills over the year. I have had English students who incorrectly answer an inference-based question because the wording of the question itself was confusing to them. Does this then mean that they are unable to infer details from the passage itself? Not necessarily, and what's more likely is I have other deficiencies that require more immediate attention. Proponents of state tests like to say that the data tells us where we need to improve, but while "numbers don't lie," they can mislead us. This can be especially frustrating when these exams are being held up as an 'accountability measure' by the government– with funding and/or possible employment implications when the tests consistently go wrong over years.

 So are state tests trash? In short: no. There will never be a perfect way to measure whether or not students have learned everything in the standard lists. I would love to see more of a written component in humanities tests, for example, so that students get more of an opportunity to flesh out what they really know, and we don't have to ask ourselves what factors went into a single choice that settled on one of three 'wrong' answers instead of the one 'right' one. But this is also fraught with problems: since analysis of writing can be very subjective no matter how hard we try to remain neutral, more writing opens up questions about the inherent biases of the graders. The multiple choice questions at least seem to provide a more objective test that produces 'harder' numbers.

Imperfect though all approaches are, we need something we can use to evaluate large masses of students in the same subject. In an ideal world, every teacher would be professional and self-directed enough to monitor how much their students actually learn and to approach their craft critically enough to make necessary changes.

We do not live in that world.

School districts nation-wide, through tough circumstances or poor leadership, are shot through with problems: complacency, nepotism, overburdened teachers, budget issues, lack of connection with their communities, high staff turnover, and teacher burnout. I don't think most schools have *all* of these problems, but it only takes a few of them to derail a culture determined to know what students have actually learned.

So I'll take the state tests as one kind of useful measure. I don't have to make them and don't have to worry about my own peculiarities and preoccupations infecting them. They also make sure I hit everything in the standards: even the stuff I find boring or irrelevant. That's a very good thing. I've already mentioned how people who think Shakespeare is boring or irrelevant are wrong. I figure that's probably true about the stuff I don't like. Somewhere out there is a great teacher who would totally prove me wrong. I have a responsibility to try and re-examine that material from *that* teacher's perspective, and to do my best to play that role for my students.

Besides, I'll let you in on a little secret: if you do your job well, your kids (that aren't irretrievably far behind) will do fine on the test. The aforementioned problems will pop up here and there, but there will be other times when you get lucky– when something that you didn't teach well gets served up as a softball question, or a question that touches on the one part of it in which you did a decent job. If you're so dang good that you didn't have a single bad unit or bad day of instruction all year, and you don't need any good luck (and teachers like this are about as common as unicorns), then I can guarantee that the issues inherent in state tests will almost never create a significant problem for you or your students.

Of course, there are other concerns. With the growth of state tests as a measure of student achievement, there is a disturbing trend emerging that sees the test results not just as one measure, but as the *only* measure of importance. This is especially true of poorly-led districts and/or ones with high numbers of failing students or bad community relationships. Among many ways this can poison a school year is the fact that state tests occur as early as April. What priority then is placed on the final six to eight weeks of instruction? That's a lot of time without a school culture behind "meaningful" work.

Pressure can also mount to "teach to the test," i.e., alter our entire instructional approach to accommodate the format of the state tests and improve the final results. I've even heard of desperate or misguided school districts dropping regular instruction for weeks before the administration of the tests in favor of 'test prep,' an insidiously simple name for what is actually a subversion of what education is supposed to be. 'Test prep' is usually focused on teaching students how to 'beat' the format of the test in ways that have nothing to do with whether or not they know the subject material.

I have no problem with "test prep" in principle: I used books and courses exactly for that purpose while trying to get higher SAT, GRE, and GRE-subject scores. Higher scores would get me more attention in a very crowded field of applicants. When one thousand very highly-skilled people need to get whittled down to one hundred, it behooves an applicant to try to get an edge. But I don't believe this has any place in public schools, especially at the expense of real instruction in subject areas. Grades 1-12 are the places in which the basic thinking skills necessary for citizenship are acquired. These numbers should not be fudged or artificially inflated to save some principal's job, especially when there is hardly enough time to cover everything in our standards as it is.

But here's the thing: I've taught in districts that were very heavily "test score-driven." I never taught to the test and I never will. And you know what? My kids have always kicked ass on the test– every single year I was under pressure for them to perform.

Whether or not you have a 'test-driven' principal or administrator is outside your control, of course. But aside from the "nuclear option" of leaving your school district, there are other things you can do: like make such obvious, measurable progress with your students that the tests take care of themselves or at least you are clearly not the problem. After all, our goal shouldn't just be "my students do well on the state test." We should have other, more specific goals for our students: more subject-specific (e.g., "My students will understand why history is important") and maybe even life-specific (e.g., "My students will know how to clearly and professionally communicate in writing" or "My students will know how to effectively work as a real team").

Before we write a single lesson or even unit plan, we need to have a look at our subject-specific standards published by our state or provided by our school, then think of the big, life-specific things we'd like kids to get out of our classes. Consider how you can encapsulate these into a few Big Goals, and then write those goals down. Any one of you who has served with TFA or a famous charter school network might be rolling your eyes right now: you've heard this before. But really. Write them down: no more than three or four, maybe even as few as two. Trust me: it's hard to make more than a couple of Big Goals happen. Write them down, read them, and re-read them. Did you capture the essence of what you want your kids to accomplish by the *end of the school year*? (Again, leave the state tests out of it)

Now ask yourself: how will I know if the kids have gotten there? For some of us, the answer for the subject-specific stuff will be as simple as looking at the list of standards and how our state breaks down what it wants students to know. If we've got a more life-specific goal, then we might need to write a few paragraphs about how success in that goal might be measured. Above all, that is the one rule governing any Big Goal we make: for it to be measurable and for us to have a clear way of evaluating whether or not the students have succeeded in learning it (and by extension, whether or not we have done our jobs well).

Now design your final exam. It doesn't have to be something completed on paper or even a computer: it's just something that adequately captures what you wrote about. If a student got an A on it, you could feel assured that the student learned and retained nearly everything you taught. And yes, before you do anything else, you are designing your final. This is hard, because it's tough to distil a whole year's worth of learning into one project/test/whatever, but I still like it better than any alternative, because it gets me doing something I learned as a TFA and KIPP teacher, and it's an enormously powerful tool: backwards planning.

In backwards planning, you always start from the end, or the end result you envision. All of your instruction then flows from that direction. When you've got that stuff you've written down, you can plan your whole year around it– every unit and in turn, every daily objective within every unit. In a way, it adds pressure to confront your standards and plan your final immediately. In taking ownership of what the final result needs to be, now you feel more responsibility to get it all taught and taught well. If a lot of the kids don't do well, there's really nowhere to hide: it's your fault. Truly looking at our standards and imagining what the students need to know by the end of the year can also be intimidating because it makes you aware of just how few days you have to get *everything* taught and assessed, while also allotting time for review.

On the other hand, backwards planning is liberating. Once you've got your standards and/or your written vision, and then have your awesome final exam planned, you can focus. "What exactly am I doing and when am I doing it?" can be an anxiety-filled question for teachers. Backwards planning forces you to answer that question and bend your skills to executing the answer in a manner that will adequately teach the kids everything they need to know. This also has a positive added side effect of making you less inclined, when you're stressed or tired, to just "give the kids something to keep them busy for a few days." Every unit you have and every daily objective you make should be working towards your end result.

About those units and objectives: keep them simple and design a sequence that lets them build on each other. Simplicity is so important, especially for inexperienced teachers. That might seem a little counterintuitive: if you're inexperienced, shouldn't you be putting loads of thought into deep and complex objectives, to make sure you cover everything that needs to be done? *To make sure you've done a GOOD job?!* I get it. I tied myself up in knots for the first few years of my career thinking this way, spending hours and hours trying to make perfect units and daily objective-driven lessons.

It was a poor use of time and an absolute burner for stress. There are so many things that can torpedo a lesson early in your career, as you are simultaneously learning about how to effectively manage a classroom and direct a year-long learning experience. Oftentimes those torpedoes are going to hit irrespective of how much time or quality you attempt to put into unit or lesson objectives. It's so tough when you stress out for hours trying to plan for good school weeks and days, then you stress out even harder when they fail, especially when you can't see the link between your planning and the failure. It's even *worse* when a lesson fails *because* of all the time you spent planning it: because it was too ambitious. It's tough when you realize you've squandered quality time; it's even tougher when quality time was not only wasted, but *counterproductive*.

So when in doubt: simplify. Make your unit objectives as brief as possible and break them down into smaller essential elements from there. Make your daily lesson objectives into a single, simple sentence that (preferably) every kid in your class can read and understand. It might even sound like something you could teach in less than fifteen minutes: good. More time for practice, re-teaching, and helping kids understand. More time for you to think about classroom management, culture, and your general level of modeling for students. If you're really reflecting on your process, you can evaluate later on and say "Ok, I could have added more to this," or "Next year, I can probably knock out these two lessons in a single day." This is a craft, after all. While it might seem like a lowering of the standard, if we aren't measurably succeeding at the 'expert' level, it's time to step back and refine our skills. I'll take a simple plan that succeeds over a deeply complex plan that fails, any day of the week.

If needed, you can add the complexity later. If you are, like I was, a TFA corps member, this can be hard to absorb. TFA teaches you that your students need to CATCH UP, RIGHT NOW, AS MUCH AS POSSIBLE. This is an excellent mission driver, but teaching is a long game, both for you and your students. You will take a big step forward if you've got a clear plan with a clear end result, from the 'macro' level ("what will my kids learn this year?") down to the 'micro' level ("what will my kids learn today?").

Don't over-think. Don't over-write. Make it happen, leave space in the schedule to correct teaching mistakes, and we can see what needs revision when we get to the end of the road. It will almost certainly be more effective than no plan or a loose idea of a plan. You also won't fall victim to the classic problem of a teacher really trying to do a great job despite all the obstacles: burnout.

MANAGE YOURSELF AND YOUR STRESS

Stress management is such an underrated part of good teaching. While I truly enjoyed the sense of mission, drive, and leadership that came with my experience in TFA and the charter school movement, I felt like my organizations (at least during my time) had much to learn in this regard. *Working hard* is classically American: studies show we spend far more hours at work than most other countries in the developed world. Some of our most prestigious professions (doctors, lawyers, business management) almost proudly advertise the early *grind* involved in the development of their newest recruits and the crazy numbers of hours and levels of stress that must be endured to succeed. While I have some problems with this attitude in general, I have special reservations about it when applied to teaching.

People under constant high levels of stress eventually take it out on someone or something. *Grinding* is hard on relationships and on any general sense of well-being. Over especially long periods, it can even be traumatic. Your students are the people who will be dealing most with the psychological consequences of your 80-hour workweeks. They are not adults who have chosen to share the grind with you. I can't tell you how many times I've heard a well-meaning, hard-working person who got into the profession because they genuinely care about children–screaming at their kids. Nearly every day. Because they are working so hard for so many hours trying to make everything perfect, and when it all falls apart in front of a room full of people, the embarrassment, resentment, and shame cause the explosion.

You owe your students an excellent education, but you also owe them dignity, respect, and a safe environment in which to learn, no matter how much trouble some of them may be giving you. You owe them reasonable teaching objectives that fit within the powers of your skill. If you are putting in 80 hour workweeks and you are still not getting any "wins" in the classroom, something needs to change, and the answer cannot be "work harder." You are not studying for exams or doing unpleasant lower-level work; you are managing rooms full of young people all day. They need leadership. It is not their fault if your plans are too ambitious for your skill.

One thing Teach for America greatly emphasized to us as new teachers was to set goals, and to make them "ambitious, but feasible." It's a laudable approach, based on the idea that if we are ambitious, even if we fall short of our ultimate goal, we'll probably accomplish more than we would have if we had set easily-reachable goals. When large numbers of our students are years behind and we desperately want to help them catch up, these kinds of goals seem especially appropriate. And really, when we are on a mission to make a difference, who doesn't want to accomplish something big? As a result, early in our careers we can emphasize ambition over feasibility– and I think that's ultimately a mistake.

A school year is a marathon rather than a sprint. When we are truly ambitious with a year-long goal, what we can feel when things go awry in the first two months of the school year is the pressure of the goal combined with its sense of inevitable failure. When we are trying to grow and get better as teachers, coming out of the beginning already carrying a sense of crushing failure is not good. Here is where the ambitious begin to spend hours and hours of their lives attempting to work their way through and catch up. As they do this, many of them begin to psychologically and spiritually deteriorate in front of their colleagues and students.

Worse still, a mentality can begin to form that it is the *students* who owe *you*. "I've been working 80 hours a week and these little shits still can't pay attention! Ungrateful!" You cannot expect your students to understand and respect your insanely unsustainable workweek. If you are failing to engage them with the joy or importance of your subject area, you are just one more boring aspect of school to them. Throwing away every hour of your waking life to be that boring will seem incomprehensible at best, contemptible at worst. This combination of attitudes in students and teacher will create a toxic environment in your classroom. When that happens: bye-bye learning and any chance at making a positive impact. Your thousands of work hours will be for nothing.

For this reason, if you are struggling with the sense of failure or are uncertain about how to even be a good teacher, I think it is vitally important to work with your mentor to set up some goals that are more on the short-term and feasible side. Get some wins, and then (very important) build on those wins in a way that turns them into habits. Take an approach in line with your strengths and what is working, with an eye to minimize the effect of your weaknesses.

To use a personal example: after I'd set my super-ambitious goals my first year, it quickly became apparent that I was struggling to manage a classroom. I was teaching what I had planned so hard to teach, and trying to address a big, obvious flaw in my classroom management by setting up strict procedures for student behavior. As weeks rolled by, behavior got better with massive stressed-out inputs from me, but learning did not; compliance with rules is not engagement in learning. Meanwhile, behavior was not improving enough to allow success for my ambitious plans. Most students complied, tuned out as I yelled a *lot*, and everyone was miserable. I was trying so hard to meet my big goals by not allowing my flaws to have an effect, that I forgot to do any of the things I was good at. As I clung to my unrealistic expectations for my plans, my palpable frustration made my classroom culture deteriorate even further. By late October, I scoured my first few months for any kind of real, systematic *wins,* and I had *none,* despite great effort, many hours, and high stress. I sank into depression.

If only I had played more to my *strengths,* and when things got tough, had some short-term, feasible goals to go with my long-term ambitious ones, things might have been different. If only I were not squandering countless hours on stuff that wasn't working, then coming in angry and stressed out every day, ready to take it out on students, then maybe I could have created a better culture. At the very least, I might have had a path with some markers showing me how much I was actually getting better.

It is important to create a sustainable balance in this process between getting better as a teacher while making a real difference, and remaining a healthy, positive human being with a life to model for your students. Modeling angry, on-the-verge-of-a-breakdown self-sacrifice is warped and inappropriate. Get a path to some winning habits, but also make that time to be a whole person– that interesting one we talked about a few chapters ago. Love the job, love your students, and remember that you aren't just a teacher of a subject, you are a teacher (through modeling and your example, if nothing else) of how to be human, and ultimately, just a human yourself.

But be careful that you also remember that…

LOVE AIN'T ENOUGH

I've written already about how important real, actual love for kids is. We all had indifferent teachers when we were in school. Whether it was a case of somebody who had been teaching a little too long or never should have been there in the first place, we remember that teacher: more vividly than a lot of our better teachers, unfortunately. An uncaring or negative teacher can have a terrible effect on children and their experience of school. Nobody wants to be that person.

Then there are the more recent educators in the data-driven movement of running schools: the people who get so caught up in the mission goals of student achievement (worthy as it is), that they lock in on the goal numbers of the *achievement* and they forget the *student*. For many teachers, schools, and even entire districts, the aforementioned state test scores become THE defining measure of a teacher that's properly invested in the job, and when this culture goes too far, school can be made into a joyless grind for kids. In one of my schools, for example, students had about 25 minutes per day of unstructured, non-instructional time, during a school day that began at 7:15 and ended at 4:15. It felt like a communist re-education gulag.

As is so often the case with rebellion, however, the push-back on data-driven culture has created a space for people to go too much in the other direction. This is especially true when it concerns students who are dealing with hard life situations. It can be so easy to say "What this child *needs* is not a 70% on a test; this child needs *love*." And you know what? That's true. But we need to be careful that we don't fully substitute love for anything and everything else. Our students need far more than love, even if we are one of the only sources of that in their lives. Our students also need *growth* to become the independent adults they should be.

Growth, academically and socially, can only come with expectations, and in *your* classroom, those expectations have to come from *you*.

Students need your leadership and professionalism– and I would argue this is especially true when they have troubled lives or are behind academically. As their teacher, you are fortunate enough to be in a position to empower them by showing them a way to be successful in something they might not have experienced success in before. Love and support are great (and my students get plenty of it from me– more on this subject later), but your ultimate responsibility is to show them how to be better at _____, and to expect that they will learn. Many of our most troubled students have more than enough people in their lives that don't expect anything of them– and that's a terrible, toxic place to be. Kids want to know they're growing, progressing, and maturing into someone upon whom the people they love can rely.

We can and should play a part in this process. We are not just observers or someone who is here to listen. We are *leaders*, and wherever our kids are when they begin their time with us, our *expectation* for every one of them should be growth in whatever facets we can assist. I've written already about how important it is to not shortchange your subject area in this regard. Your subject and how to think about it, how you expect people to treat each other, how everyone approaches writing, etc.– all things dealing with humans and knowledge in your classroom are part of the Way. They represent something important in which a student can grow towards adulthood under your guidance.

If you are going to be any kind of true positive influence in a child's development, as opposed to just a nice person they once knew, it is vitally important to recognize that this *is* a part of love. I can remember holding up a pencil in front of my seventh graders once, explaining to them how powerful and terrible writing was– because for many of them, what they wrote and released, whether it be a job application, a college essay, or an online comment, would become an instant snapshot by which those who didn't know them would judge their entire character. From day one, I *expected* that in my writing class, their pencils and what they wrote with them would be treated with this level of respect— as if a stranger with the power to influence their lives were reading *them* for the first time. This was pretty heavy.

Now did I expect that everyone would be writing at an advanced level by the end of the year? Did I expect everyone to give 100 percent effort, all the time? No. These goals would have been absurdly unrealistic, especially given the challenges many of my students faced and the academic shortcomings they had from years of going to poorly-run, poorly-supported schools. But I had done a writing diagnostic in the first few days, and observed the level of contempt with which my kids treated writing. Through that contempt I could see the pathetically low expectations other people had for their writing up to this point in their lives. I mean, it was ridiculous: the doodles and graffiti all over the paper, the barely-legible or illegible handwriting, even in kids who clearly had the chops to write better, the lack of names or identification.

I thought: *this has to change*. Even down to the pencils. I have had so many well-meaning colleagues who give away hundreds of pencils all year, and I think it's nuts. "They're going through so much; I can't expect they'll have a pencil every day."

Yes. Yes you can. And you *should*–especially when you gave them the damn pencil!

Pencils represent the simplest and most elemental way for students to show mastery of material and to express themselves as individuals. In my class, they were the only things absolutely necessary to get the job done. If I can't expect them to keep track of the one thing necessary to do anything in my class, how can I possibly expect anything else?

Sooner or later, life will require all of our students to keep track of something or other, no matter how challenging their existence might be.

Now, there might be a process here. We might need to break the students in with a new procedure and give them a few chances. Perhaps this means a system for tracking pencils is necessary. Maybe it just means a class culture initiative like mine was necessary. Or it could just be something to personally address with a few kids. But let me tell you: if you don't think a twelve year old can handle expectations around pencils, you are criminally underestimating that twelve year old. When you let that twelve year old lose three different pencils of yours like it's nothing, you send a very powerful message that they don't have to give a shit about *anything,* much less school or what you have to teach. When you give away that fourth pencil, you send a very powerful message (through your actions, which are much more meaningful than any words you might have on the subject) that A) what they accomplish with that pencil has no real importance, or B) that if there's any kind of real importance to it, someone will always be there to make sure they get the basics complete. Those aren't the kind of precedents I want to set in the first week of my class. They're toxic for class, but they're also toxic for life. I felt comfortable expecting growth in that area even among my most challenged students.

This did not mean I started yelling at people and shaming kids over pencils and handwriting. After the aforementioned talk about how serious the implications were around their writing, I chose to use the way in which I'd built relationships with students and my class culture in general to generate an ultra-nerd new ritual: a call-and-response routine to start every writing class, centered on pencils. My students open every day with something to do immediately as they enter the classroom (what some would call bell work or a do first). For me, this is an excellent way to get them focused and working right away, usually on something I've already taught that will link with today's lesson. I give them a short amount of time to do it: usually less than 5 minutes after the bell rings, and when it's over, I open class. In this case, after time reminders, I would simply say "pencils up." Every student would then hold their pencils aloft. I had a short script: I would call on a student at random and ask them "Why is this pencil/pen important?" And the answer that could begin class had to be "Because this, to the world, is our most powerful voice."

That might sound like corny chickenshit to you, and in *your* class, that might be true, but when students aren't meeting basic expectations, I urge you to use whatever means available to *you* to find things about class culture that you can change, and begin to raise expectations in a positive way. Mine had the good added side effect of allowing me to see with a quick glance if everyone had their pencils, and to quietly address any pencil issue right at the start of class. It also ingrained in the kids that they had to come prepared, or they would be directly confronted with their lack of preparation immediately. Many students lose or forget pencils (consciously or unconsciously) to have a convenient excuse for not engaging with class.

Will students test boundaries like these? Absolutely. I had other methods for dealing with these tests, routinized and customized to my class and the culture I promoted. There is no cookie-cutter solution for every test of your expectations that you'll get. Your kids will bring behaviors to you that are the result of so many different variables: home lives, previous school experiences, peer groups, levels of confidence within your subject, etc. There are certain basic levels of expectations you will set for your class that are shaped by your personality and class culture; then there are others you can customize to the group of children you have in any given academic year. The important thing is to have expectations, and to expect that while maybe not everyone knows how to meet them right away, everyone will grow enough to meet them quickly.

Growth for everyone in your class is the most important thing.

THE NATURAL LAWS FOR ALL HUMANS IN YOUR CLASSROOM

I have spent most of this little book writing about things you should have in place before you even teach a lesson, if possible. Your mindset, your appreciation of what's possible, and your work on yourself is such an important part of being truly successful in this game. These things can and should evolve as you learn more: about your subject, your rapport with kids, and what makes *your* class more engaging and fun. This evolution should never stop. Like the great swordsmen know in the old samurai stories, there is always another move to master. But what about your classroom and your lessons? What happens in the room where the execution of teaching is going on– *the room where it happens?*

The truth is that you are the Creator of your own little world, whether you acknowledge it or not. The more you actively shape the "natural laws" for everything in your classroom, the smoother and easier teaching will be. I put "natural laws" in quotes because of course this is not the literal truth, but it's useful to think of your classroom in this way: that every time a certain "x" behavior, positive or negative, happens, there will always be "y" result. And I do mean *every* time– as close to a real natural law as you can bring it.

Contrary to popular belief, students appreciate structure. Not in the sense of punitive rules with disciplinary consequences, which is unfortunately what many people think structure means; but in the sense of knowing exactly what to expect from their environment and their leaders. Our kids have a keen sense of what's fair and just, and will often adjust their own thinking and mindset based on what they see from adults in this regard. True fairness and justice is blind and consistent, and applies to all people in your classroom.

Naturally, this must start with you. I say naturally, but it's sad how often this is *not* the case in school. I have seen many teachers who expect deference, respect, engagement, and high effort from students, without question, but fail to live up to that expectation themselves. If you are one of those people that says "Well, I'm the adult, and they're the kids, so they need to know there is a difference," *you* need to know that this idea is flawed, especially for a leader of young people. Kids learn best through modeling. You are not a stranger to your students, or their boss. It's true that the classroom in some ways models employment, but in real life, if you were an authoritarian, inconsistent, or hypocritical boss, your students would have the choice to quit. They cannot quit *you*. And you are their teacher, in more ways than just your subject, whether you want to admit it or not. Why would you want to model such behavior? It would be teaching hypocrisy: maybe not in a formal lesson, but in action.

Aside from the moral problem of being a hypocrite, this is simply an ineffective way to run a classroom or build the relationships required for that classroom to be successful. When children perceive that you are just another "do as I say, not as I do" adult, not only will they not trust you, they will view whatever else you may be trying to teach them in the same tarnished way. Any student not already motivated and engaged in your subject material and/or school itself will have an even harder time bridging the gap. Think about it: when have you ever heard "I'm the adult; they're the kids" as a proudly used explanation of success? It's nearly always the defensive explanation of a failure– in a classroom culture, in parenting, or any other situation in which kids don't meet the expectations of adults and the adult in question is frustrated.

It's that cliche again, but kids respect an adult who can lead by example. If you don't want students to yell in your classroom, you must never yell. If you're going to put up a sign in your classroom about how respect is the most important expectation, you *must* respect your students at all times. It can be so easy when a kid is in the throes of stupid rebellion, or trying to give you or someone else a hard time, to use the weapon of your seasoned wit and experience to publicly cut them down. This is always a mistake. If you've seen Star Wars, imagine Luke's final temptation: to cut down the Emperor. He knows he must not give in to hate, and so refuses: winning not the short-term present battle, but the much more important battle for his soul. That has to be you.

The minute you publicly cut down a student, you do damage to the leadership bond and credibility you have with the entire class. It's using the Dark Side to win a specific little scenario, but one that casts a shadow on your trustworthiness as an adult to truly lead your students to better things. This is true *even if the entire class feels the student deserved it.* As adults, we all laugh/sneer/lose patience with "kid drama" and how short-sighted and immature it can be. We imagine ourselves to be above it, and as teachers, we absolutely should be. When you cut a student down to size in reaction to their behavior, you are *not* above that short-sighted and immature fray; you are right in the thick of it, slinging weapons. Everyone in your class will be aware of that fact and it will be a destabilizing influence.

The standard of leadership by example applies to all expectations for your class; not just behavior. One of my other favorites is the one that often goes "all of us/all students will learn." Are *you* modeling learning? I've mentioned this already above, but this goes beyond expanding your knowledge within your subject area. Do you publicly reveal the moments when you feel like you've learned something about teaching or how to be a human, even from your students? We have a basic human desire to make ourselves appear as the experts in front of these kids, but it's actually a very powerful thing when we show the ways in which we're not, especially if it involves them.

Whenever questions, experimentation, or feedback from my students changes something about my instruction, I always let them know. Contrary to what you might think, it doesn't lead to widespread ideas like "this guy doesn't know what he's doing!" I've already established I know what I'm doing through my subject mastery, genuine passion for kids, and all the planning I've put into my lessons and assessments. As a result, I'm not flailing or fumbling or changing things left and right. When I change something, it's unusual. When the kids know they've been a part of it, they feel how empowered they are– that they are an active part of the process of learning in the class. And they respect it.

You might have a better idea about how to do things than a kid 19 times out of every 20, but it's such a missed opportunity if you don't give them the credit on the one time out of twenty. "I'm supposed to be the teacher!! It has to at least look like I know the best answer 20 out of every 20!" No. Everyone, including you, knows you don't always have the right idea. By opening up when the kids have a better one, you not only invest them more in class, you strengthen all the other times when you know you've got the right idea and you choose to hold the line. After all, you've already proven you listen to students and aren't trying to pretend to be perfect out of pride: if you're holding the line, it must *really* mean you believe you've got the best interests of everyone in mind.

Being open to learning from the feedback of others extends beyond the kids in your class, by the way. As much as I'll hear teachers admit to not being perfect, many people seem to hate visits from school administrators or anyone else to their class. Why? Are we hiding something? Whatever you're hiding, the kids can see it. Most of us already get the absurdly sweet deal of the visit that's used for our professional evaluation having to be scheduled with us. I know of many colleagues who use this reality to make a "really good" lesson for that day, and therefore game the system. Do you think your students don't see the difference? Here again, we are modeling bad human traits: dishonesty, kissing up to the boss, and indifference to our profession.

A lesson during a visit from the principal should look like any other lesson you have. This is why I always tell my administrators to visit my class literally whenever they feel like it, as often as they like. When you do this, you win in two ways: 1) any flaws you've got will hopefully get noticed and get the proper feedback. You'll win the trust and actual respect of your boss. More importantly, 2) you send a powerful message to your students: *this is who we are, this is what we do, and I don't mind anybody seeing it. We all learn here.* The kids will have it proven to them that both the passion and the routines you've implemented were designed with the toughest audience in mind. There will also be the added benefit of those routines being present: since it's clearly not a "special" day, every kid in class will obviously know exactly what is going on and be comfortable with what their role in it is supposed to be. This is a chunk of most teaching professional observations.

Welcoming constructive criticism from any source at any time has so many other benefits, as well. In my fourth year of teaching I was at a KIPP Charter school and struggled mightily with the workload and number of hours required. I had some very legitimate gripes with the school about the use of teacher hours, as it turned out: My KIPP region made streamlining teacher time a priority two years later. I also had an increasingly antagonistic relationship with my first KIPP principal. Our school was in chaos: we had lost or fired nine people by January (with a total teaching staff of 23). Having (I thought) proven my ability at my previous school in Tulsa, I was feeling angry, fed up, and high on my horse about my position in the school.

To make matters worse, KIPP had a standing policy of administrators doing walk-throughs whenever they wished. I was getting visits more and more frequently as I struggled to meet my principal's expectations, and ultimately wound up having a rather ominous series of "sit-downs" with him about how to improve. At this point, pride, stress, and self-righteousness had nearly conquered any possibility of me listening to KIPP feedback. I had to actively fight to swallow it long enough to give his words a chance. Fortunately for me, I didn't give in to all of my "justifiable" emotions. His feedback for how to overhaul my class proved to be the second real turning point in my development!

He even modeled how to do it for me, both in the preparation and execution of the ideas. The kids, by the way, knew what this looked like: that their teacher was *in trouble*, which was of course horribly awkward and humbling for me at first.

BUT I LEARNED, and quite publicly. It wound up being an incredible way to show my students: *hey, I'm a learner, too* and live out one of the unofficial laws of my class, which was that when someone is giving you thoughtful feedback, you absorb it, think it over, and if necessary, adjust– no matter who that person may be.

After all, we are never too *right* to learn something from a seasoned colleague in the game, AND the basic principles of what he and I hashed out in those heated moments are ones I still use in my planning every day. It's something I'd like to share with you in your own planning.

STRUCTURE AND PROCEDURE:
YOU THOUGHT THEY WERE BORING, BUT YOU WERE WRONG

I can remember how preoccupied I was as an early-career teacher with trying to make interesting lessons. Whatever students would say about me, I didn't want them to say I was boring, or that class was the same thing over and over. Even when I had cut my instructional time down for more reading and analysis, I still spent many hours wringing my hands about that time. *How can I keep this fresh? How can I do different things?*

My first KIPP principal radically challenged my avenue of thinking. He asserted that part of my problem was that the kids didn't know what to expect every day, so they never really got into a groove. I had no definable process for how my class worked, and no clear transitions. He detailed suggestions for me, which came to this: my class would run by the same process nearly every day, and if it were ever going to run in a different way, even that should be planned, practiced, and have its own clear "look" and "feel." Basically, I would develop my own brand of classroom teaching and procedure that would be instantly recognizable to my students.

This approach was comprehensive. My mode of presentation was PowerPoint, beginning with a critical thinking question that transitioned into my lesson material, that transitioned into guided practice, that transitioned into independent practice for the students. We ran all student work through packets, and he even had me develop a format for how my packets looked (the border, font, layout– even my own militant star graphic in the top right corner), and worked with me on how to use the packet every day (I realize most schools have limited print budgets; we didn't, but we also didn't have consistent curriculum material, and the packets were intended to at least partly make up for that fact– the key here is the element of daily consistency in what the students do).

The main idea here is not that PowerPoint and packets are the best way to teach: they were the best way in *that* school for me to develop a consistent way to 'do my thing' with *those* students, such that the classroom became a well-oiled machine. I had about three different formats for how a learning day could run, and 90% of the time they ran on one of those formats. I got some student grumbles over time, but the trade-off was well worth it. Everyone in class came to know how a Kruger learning day worked, and so could shift effortlessly into the learning itself.

I think of it as akin to a game like chess or a sport like wrestling. There are levels to how each is played. With constant practice, certain elements that had to be thought through in the beginning become easy, then completely automatic. As chess players, we begin with trying to figure out how the pieces move, then how to move them efficiently to open up opportunities at multiple points, then how to anticipate implications. With experience, the movement of pieces, opening combinations, and the possibilities of the board become completely automatic. Freed up from having to think about them, we can think bigger and deeper, many moves ahead, anticipating the reactions of our specific opponents in specific situations.

Similarly, in wrestling, we struggle with how to execute takedowns and defend against them, how to execute pinning combinations that work for us, and how to spend energy. Eventually the speed and efficiency with which we execute these things becomes instinctive, freeing up our thoughts for deeper and more decisive moves that accomplish their aims in combination before the opponent can gather himself to react effectively. If you enter a chess or wrestling match thinking "what am I doing today?" you are unlikely to achieve anything impressive.

Students should not be learning a different way to 'play your game' every day. Neither should they be wondering what they're doing on any given day. The basics of your lesson structure and the different kinds of thinking and work required of students should be something they master through practice. With these things automatic, all brain power can be directed toward the deep thinking you want to accomplish. Student questions of "how do we do this?" should be reserved for the deepest and most difficult things you want them to accomplish. The quicker you can move most parts of your classroom to a place where they no longer require teacher instructions or directions, the better.

I saw the difference after a few weeks in my own classroom. Students got used to exactly how to do my bell work, such that the instant they entered class, they sat down and began it, knowing immediately what to do. Similarly, I would transition them into a question about the book we were reading, and use the discussion to move us into the thinking skill for the day's lesson. Meanwhile, after a few days, the kids all knew to have their books right there on the desk for reference and an automatic transition into reading. All I'd have to say was "here we go," and everyone would open their books to where we left off. The students also knew that each day would have a few critical questions that I would reveal one at a time on the board, with space in their packet to answer and explain. These questions would key on the day's skill, but would often extend to other reading skills that had been learned. The final and highest question would always synthesize multiple skills and require more time.

Eventually, the kids literally had to think about nothing but critical engagement with the reading they were doing. It became so automatic that as I read out loud, many of them would already be anticipating what the questions would be or what developments in the text were significant enough to require them. This was magic for me. As a reading teacher, I might be teaching them on any given day about making good predictions, for example, but everyone would automatically consider the whole plot, character traits, the cause-and-effect relationships in the story, the word choice of the author and how to infer conclusions from it. The students constantly reinforced skills I had already taught them with no direct words from me or forced and isolated practice for them. Once they had mastered the basics of my instructional game, they were free to progress as critical thinkers.

Throwing your students a curveball, changing up the routine, or surprising them with something totally different should be reserved for when those processes are so firmly in place, the deep thinking can quickly be picked up along with the delight of something new. I rarely ever show movies in my classroom: I generally regard them as a lazy way many teachers "take a break" from instruction and a too-easy excuse for students to tune out. After teaching Stephen King's *Rita Hayworth and the Shawshank Redemption* to a great group of kids, (who simply knocked that unit out of the park) I decided to show the movie, pausing periodically for discussion and questions. I wanted to present it as a story on its own merit and as a way to compare written and visual art forms. It was awesome: the students treated the film as they did every story they'd read with me. The thinking and discussion was just as deep and rich because we had all proven we could be trusted with our part in it. 'Something new' should be a level-up, not a whole new game.

And who wants to invent a whole new game over and over, anyway? With the enormous relief of "how am I going to deliver this?" more or less answered, I could focus on improving other things– things that have critical importance for a deeply successful classroom.

INSTRUCTION FOR ALL

As my career progressed and I had more and more kids engrossed in stories, I was feeling pretty good about myself and ignoring a couple of red flags I should have noticed earlier. I had all kids quiet in seats (total compliance with classroom behavior expectations) and the vast majority paying attention. This did not mean, however, that everybody was learning like they should have been!

As my manager (and future second KIPP principal) pointed out to me, I had many kids in class that were not misbehaving, but were zoning out for chunks of the reading. I had others who, because of English not being their native language or just generally limited vocabulary, were struggling to understand deeper things in the plot, even if they were following the general plot well. Still others occasionally struggled to understand the connection between the thinking skill I had taught and how to use it with the text– my lesson didn't "click" for them.

My initial response to this was defensive (my brain was thinking something along the lines of: "I've only got so much time to deal with all the different learning abilities in a classroom of 27 kids! JEEZ!!"), but once again, fortunately for me, I took a deep breath and took a crash course on her suggestions. What I had was the *next* big turning point in my career! She had a few tweaks for both introducing new material and practicing it with kids, and I'd like to share those with you.

For my new instruction, she reminded me that I need to think of all the types of students in my classroom, and use vocabulary that *everyone* could understand. She didn't mean to never use big or tough words, especially in practice when raising comprehension levels is going to require some challenges: she just meant to refrain from it while teaching a brand new thinking process or thinking skill, especially when using the screen or the board. There are words I naturally use that were going right over the heads of my English Language Learners and my low-comprehension students. The material was already going to be challenging for them; why make it even harder with an introduction that itself is hard to understand? *"Well, they should know that already"* is not an acceptable answer when you've got a class full of kids with widely different abilities. Whether they *should* or not, you are the teacher: help 'em out! It's not that hard to think about the words you use and adjust them accordingly.

For practice time, she said to consider using groups and breaking the class up into chunks of time, so there's opportunity for discussion. I *loved* this adjustment. Before, I would always periodically stop reading and ask questions about the text, with wait time for answers. When I wanted to challenge a kid, I would call on them, and if they were confused, give them leading questions to try and help them recall parts of the text/what I'd taught until they could get to a good conclusion themselves. What would happen, however, is that I came to recognize the kids that clearly weren't going to be able to answer the questions, and were always confused no matter how much time or help they had, and I wouldn't ask them. I would try to check in with them during the time students had to independently practice, but this brought forward a couple of new problems.

For one thing, during limited time for checking in, I was trying to get a student caught up on a whole class-worth of reading and thinking. Even if things went relatively smooth, the student would be scrambling to complete the practice or the writing on time. This is not good for the portion of the lesson where the student is supposed to be putting everything together so it sticks for the future. Additionally, there were nearly always too many of these kinds of students for this kind of check-in. I would have four kids who really needed it and I'd only have time for one.

As per my boss's suggestion, I grouped kids in fours. This was easy in my classroom at the time, because every student was seated at a table with enough room for four. Even after I left this arrangement, however, I continued to use groups of four with student desks, either by permanently bringing them together or simply seating kids in such a way that they could always turn and talk to each other when necessary. When I would pause reading (or guided practice) to ask a big question, I'd let the groups of four discuss it and give them adequate time to do so. This served a few different functions at once.

Most importantly, my kids that 'got it' could help the kids who didn't 'get it.' Sometimes these were friendly relationships where one kid knew the other enough to correctly and informally diagnose what the problem was (like, for example, the kid was zoning out a little yesterday because he and his girlfriend broke up, so he just needs a quick summary of how yesterday connects to today). Sometimes these were more professional relationships in which I required the group to have everybody capable of answering a cold call when discussion time was over, so they could put their heads together and get to the right stuff through collaboration. Sometimes, my higher-level English Language Learners could explain the difficult English language in the text to their lower-level classmates, often using Spanish to fill in context in a way I never could for that individual.

This also gave me time to work the room: early in the year, to walk the room and observe how the discussions were going, what the dynamics were between the kids, and making note of any possible changes to the groups that might be needed. As time went by and I came to trust how different groups had gelled, I could devote more and more time to checking in with the really struggling students to make sure they were more adequately prepared for independent practice right when it started. I could also check in with other groups and kids, just to see how they were/what they were thinking. If a group was really doing well, I might talk with them and push them a little further with extension questions, while praising their high ability. Discussion time was awesome both for reinforcing instruction and for building relationships. I spread the check-ins around, reinforcing most of all that I care about *everybody*.

One of my initial doubts about it was that the laziest kids would leech off the hardest-working kids. To get ahead of this, I decided not to grade this work. I dealt with them very publicly and answers were required, but the time for grading was later. When it is time to do something with a grade (which in my class means to independently show me your understanding of the concepts, so I can know whether you've learned or not), there is no discussion. It's the only time my classroom is completely silent.

Of course, there are always a few recalcitrant students who resent (for various reasons) a class process that requires them to do anything challenging. I would check in with these kids regularly, treating each time as a true opportunity to get to the root of their misunderstandings. I would never reveal annoyance at their repeated disengagement– so often disengaged students want the easier road of blaming their disengagement on some issue they imagine they have with you. I do my best to never allow this dynamic to develop. My first priority is always to deal with ignorance.

Finally, I look for those hard-working, fully engaged students not just to praise and push them further, but to make sure (to the best of my ability) that they are not in a miserable situation where they are unwillingly doing all of the intellectual heavy lifting for the rest of the group. Some of my kids actually enjoy being an ambassador for the stories (or for what I'm trying to teach) enough that they don't mind being an unofficial junior teacher for their group. But I want to be alert for the ones who want less than that burden, and to change the situation accordingly. Having spent all of middle school as a relentlessly bullied runt-nerd, I know the frustration of being told I "just need to work it out" with some jerk who's been put in my group. Sometimes it's not a fair thing to say, so I circulated the room constantly, checking in with different groups and people at different times.

The results of my first real try with this were amazing. I was teaching an 8th grade history course of about ninety five total kids, and I had twelve special education students, thirty five English Language Learners, and a vast majority of kids two years or more below reading comprehension grade level. Despite this, ninety-four percent of my students passed their Texas STAAR Test, with greater than one third of them scoring higher than eighty-five percent on the exam. **AND** we had a great time doing it! I had learned how to use not just my own brain to facilitate instruction, but to harness the awesome potential of the other brains in the room. The students were empowered and enriched by the experience, and I was *less* stressed.

You might notice something else: modifying instruction, chunked lessons and practice, frequent check-ins, and preferential seating all sound like something straight off an IEP (special education Individual Education Plan). You would be right! My manager was a special education ace prior to her time in school administration and sought to impart to me the great mission of her field: that instruction can reach *all* students of *all* abilities. Contrary to what some might think, I did not have to dumb down instruction and practice or spend an inordinate amount of time with struggling students. On the contrary, I actually improved relationships with all of my students, while keeping rigorous standards. And if I could do it, any teacher can.

GRADING

State tests and other big assessments are one way to measure how well you've done your job. What about for the students? For many of them, how the grade looks is the most important thing: far more important than any abstract idea of whether or not they've learned anything. Who can blame them? Our culture reinforces the idea that grades are the stats by which they get permission to get to the next level, and there is buy-in for that idea–from the most driven Ivy League hopeful to the most cynical child's acknowledgement that a diploma is very often the bottom-line requirement for whatever career they want.

While I've tried to show that I'm a strong advocate for passionately demonstrating the importance of your subject area such that every kid connects with that for its own sake, I'm also a realist. You can't win 'em all. Either way, you need a good, consistent standard by which you can show them whether or not they're completing what needs to be done for whatever goals they have. Ultimately this means that a student's final grade should be one hundred percent the grade they have earned, and the measure of what they have learned.

For that to be true, you need to be careful with what you decide to grade. Anything I grade is a completely authentic assessment of whether a child has truly absorbed and synthesized what I've taught, either over a few days or an entire unit or group of units. The bigger the synthesis and retention required, the heavier the weight of the grade on their final average. A quick quiz of a few days' worth of material should not be worth the same as an essay requiring a whole unit's worth of knowledge, for example. Just completing an assignment or participating in an activity, are not formally grade-able in my classes at all.

Class participation can represent a student who truly understands what you've taught, but this is not always the case. It becomes especially problematic when students are otherwise struggling but perceive that participation can improve their grade. You'll get plenty of participation from these students: but is it quality? How do you evaluate the quality in a fair and consistent way? If it's just about participating, then there is no difference between the student making an insightful contribution and the student who is just raising their hand and desperately trying to parrot something you've said to get his 'grade' ticket punched. But if you don't have a formal method for evaluating the quality of participation, you invite inconsistency and playing favorites (or accusations to this effect) on your part. It's only fair for students to know exactly how and why they received the grades they got.

Completion grades suffer from the same problems. You are going to have plenty of kids who will complete the assigned work you give them as quickly as possible. I can remember doing this myself as a student! When completion was the standard, I often blew through things with the minimum possible work. The end result was questionable at best. Poorly-done work or things completed without an understanding of the learning objectives are functionally worthless. When you move the bottom line away from learning and into participating and completing, you dumb down your entire class.

Don't get me started on homework. I can understand wanting to grade homework: the thinking goes that if you don't attach a grade to homework, no one will bother doing it. I see it the other way: when you send work outside of your class and attach a grade to its completion, you send an open invitation to cheat, copy, or harness the evil powers of the internet to get it done. Sadly, the kids who need the practice the most are often the ones who don't bother completing the homework *even when cheating is easy.* Others just cheat. And who can blame them? If they don't already have a full understanding of what you've taught, to what extent can the practice actually help them? And if they do have a full understanding of what you've taught, why is the extra practice required?

Homework has a place for students (and/or their parents) who genuinely want extra practice. In my experience, these students constitute a small minority. When I've been required to assign and grade homework on a course-wide scale, most of the quality work done with diligence and effort (amid a sea of half-baked garbage, incomplete work, and flagrant cheating) is completed by children who are invested enough in class to fear the effect of blowing off homework on their high grades. Worse, for the students who could really use the boost to their average, homework zeroes become an anchor that drags it down even further.

This brings me to one of the few things I genuinely don't enjoy about my career: the inevitable deluge of questions, emails, and phone calls I get during the last few weeks of every semester by (or on behalf of) failing students. One could boil the message of all of them down to one basic question: how can we fudge things to get this final grade to passing? Can we turn in this giant stack of missing work? Can we get extra credit? WHAT CAN WE DO? It's deeply frustrating. It brings me face to face with the dumbing down of education in this country and the decreasing value of anything (including diplomas) 'earned' through that education.

The high school diploma was supposed to certify that a student had learned the basic critical thinking and other skills necessary for citizenship and adulthood. It's hard to get a job without one because it's supposed to be. Somewhere along the line, a lot of us have lost the real reason for its existence, and substituted the short-term practical idea that if a diploma is required for most jobs, then we need to get one in the hands of as many kids as possible. Of course, there are more insidious forces at work here as well. Since the advent of accountability measures that tie school ratings and sometimes government funding to graduation rates, gaming the system by school administrators is inadvertently incentivized. If there's a stack of junk one of your students can turn in late that will artificially inflate their average to passing, your principal might require you to accept it. Aside from often being an enormous waste of everyone's time and a poor substitute for actual learning, it doesn't say much for your class when this kind of greasing the gears is possible.

For this reason I think it is important to tie as much grading as possible to assessments that can be completed under your direct supervision. For this to be completely fair, you need to start the year prepared with a very clear grading policy of what is graded, and how and why it is graded. If you are grading writing often, as I am, have a formal rubric, explained and accessible to all students at all times, for how the writing earns points. Have a clear policy around deadlines for assessments missed due to school absence: this is something I'm only just coming to grasp. How do the students go about making up the work in a way that ensures integrity and how long do they have to complete the late work? This might require some imagination: perhaps a teaching friend has a spare desk your student can use while you teach your class, or you can secure permission from teachers or administrators for the student to come into your class at a different time. The bottom line is that consistency and high expectations are important in all things, and grading should be no different.

RELATIONSHIPS AND "RESPECT"

I've touched on this topic in relation to a few other themes, but I want to discuss it in its own right. Every single individual interaction you have with students is a "teachable moment." I do not mean that you should therefore be seeking to 'educate' or 'impart a lesson' with everything you do. Besides making you insufferable to kids, that would also make you powerfully inauthentic. What I mean is that in *every* interaction you have with kids, you are modeling adulthood and all of the maturity, professionalism, and humanity that is supposed to go with it. Quite aside from your actual lessons, I regard this to be some of the most important *teaching* you will ever do: modeling respect for the important things. There is a balance to strike, and it's a rough one.

On the one hand, you must model professionalism: there are instructional goals your class must meet, and fairness for all students in the expectations and direction of your class. You must resemble blind justice and even something divine in this: you've got to be *above* your students in a palpable way if you expect to be credible in your leadership. It's an important part of your real authority. The rules in the student handbook, your college diploma, and whatever expectations you put on your classroom wall are actually counterfeit authority. In your classroom, your students will only respect them insomuch as you continually model the reason why they're worthy of that respect.

This sucks, because divinity and blind justice have a couple of things in common: they're fundamentally inhuman. When our other loved ones make a mistake, we can get away with indulging them if the situation is right. Not in your class. When that beloved student who has never made a mistake for you before tearfully breaks down with an understandable reason for why she cheated on an assignment, you can empathize, but that consequence you've committed to and applied to other students must still apply. Conversely, when you more or less *know* that another sneaky student has cheated, but you have no way within the structure you've created to *prove it,* you've got to grade it as if it were purely their work. *Fairness*, the ultimate measure for any young person's esteem of an adult and any student's respect for a teacher, must be omnipresent.

On the other hand, you must always be watching and waiting for those times when you can be utterly and profoundly vulnerable and human, without undermining justice and fairness. When you can tell a student is having a bad day, and find that moment later in the hallway to ask about it, when that student won't feel awkward because of the presence of other kids. To calmly listen to kids when they have a problem: even when they think that problem is you or your class. Most importantly, to be secure enough to own up when you have made a mistake, and to do so publicly.

I can recall an incident my first year in charter school. We had a student who was a frequent behavior challenge, enough that he had earned his umpteenth "lunch detention," my school's standard punishment for major behavior infractions. While sitting at detention, the offending students had to complete a written reflection on why they were in detention, and the school had a labor-sharing system for which teachers were on duty to supervise the completion of these reflections (I'll leave my opinion of this system for another time). It was my day, and given that I'd had a tough morning already, I wasn't exactly looking forward to overseeing lunch detention.

This young man (somewhat predictably) refused to complete his reflection, and this led to some heated back-and-forth between the two of us. I grew angry and unpleasant enough that he eventually began work on it– almost certainly to end the stressful ordeal of me confronting him. As I walked away, I noticed my limbs trembling, I was so worked up. I knew that I hadn't been good, no matter how I *wanted* to look at it.

Whatever, went my first, defensive thought. *Working here is tough and kids like him make it even tougher. He deserved it.*

At that thought, I pulled up short. No. No, he doesn't.

You are supposed to be the teacher: the *adult.* Does he have the slightest understanding of how many stressful hours you've worked this week? No. He's only fourteen! And, for all you know, *he's* had a really rough morning, and it probably started way before he boarded the bus for school. In any event, I knew I had done wrong, and whatever the circumstances, it was an absolute requirement for me to apologize on the spot.

I approached the student and gently asked to speak to him. When he agreed to do so, I said absolutely nothing about his behavior, looked him right in the face and apologized for getting visibly angry. I explained that I'd let stress get the better of me and it wasn't ok, and that it was important he knew that it wasn't ok. I was sorry. And you know what? In a moment I can still picture, this kid's face visibly brightened in relieved surprise and he said "It's ok." With a smile, he added "I'm sorry, too!" It was awesome, and a turning point in our relationship. I had to swallow a big gulp of my pride to make that moment happen, but I'm glad I did. We all want our kids (not to mention ourselves) to be able to own up to a mistake: don't blow an opportunity to *show* how it's done, as opposed to just *saying* you expect kids to do it.

One other example worth mentioning: I have a standing guideline in my class that when independent writing begins, all talking must cease. The function here is to prevent cheating, of course. Well, my first year of high school teaching, I was conducting a unit on Shakespeare's *Macbeth* and delighted with the progress some of my football player students had made. Part of the instant buy-in for these boys, I think, was my own shaven head and clear passion for athletics and training. As silence fell, I had one of them ask me a football-related question, and I happily addressed it. I really enjoy authentic connections with students on things other than just class, after all.

After briefly addressing football, I started my patrol of the class, walking around so as to be available for answering questions and also to be everywhere at once, as much as possible. I had a fairly new student in my class, only in our school for the last three weeks or so. She had arrived under odd circumstances and was a unique kid. Up to this point she had been excellent during our reading of the play, and quiet. This left me completely unprepared for her reaction when I noticed her whispering, looked right at her, and put my finger to my lips (the sshhh gesture).

"You know, I think it's really interesting," (she said loudly to the total silence of my class) "that you think talking about football is ok, but I can't answer a quick question about where one of the text quotes is."

Shots fired!!

There were so many ways to react to this remark. I had many bad ones bubbling up almost immediately: I felt insulted. Come *on*, kid. You've been here long enough to see I really try to run a fair class. You're going to pounce on me and try to make a point over this harmless football exchange? But that was nonsense, really. When I put myself in her shoes, here are these jocks talking about football, and this jock-looking teacher is playing favorites and not holding the line. I had certainly seen that before. When I was in high school, I always hated how the coach teachers treated the jocks differently. My situation wasn't the same– if those guys had turned in poorly-done work, they'd have been feeling the hammer as badly as anyone else, but how would she know that?

And most importantly, *she was right.* According to my own very clear procedures, I was being inconsistent. So I did what I had to do. I called the entire class to attention, and said that I had just been called out for talking about football and then hypocritically telling someone else to stay on-task, and that it was absolutely correct. I even made a point to say that "Do as I say, not as I do" is garbage and that no adult should hold a kid to a standard they won't keep themselves.

Conventional thinking might say that I had humiliated myself and the kids now had a green light to say whatever they wanted to me. Nothing could have been further from the truth. If anything, it *reinforced* the high expectations for my class, because the kids could see I'd even hang *myself* out to dry to show how important they were. What she shot down was not me personally, it was my hypocrisy and non-academic behavior. Now the kids were *less* inclined to call me out, because they fully trusted that I valued universal high expectations and would never willingly say or do anything unfair. And of course, the moment was a relationship-builder with the new kid and a powerful statement to all of my kids that coach or no coach, no jock was getting special treatment in my class.

There was another, even better benefit to this as well. Kids, especially young adults, need to test their critical faculties and know when they have correct, original ideas. We repeat the mantras to them all the time: *think for yourself, be yourself, make your own way*, but when it's time to pay a price: in obedience, in classroom efficiency, in order, or (heaven forbid) in a measure of our own pride, we reverse course and say the opposite. "Do as I say!" "This isn't the time or place for a question like that." "Here are the answers: study them and make sure you put them down on the test."

And you know what? In so many ways, we, the adults, know better and more than they do. Everything from our biological brain development to our life experience puts us ahead of them. BUT, we need to be vigilant for that one time (even out of ten or twenty) when a kid exercises independent critical thinking and is correct in a way we are not (or have not yet revealed). Acknowledging that moment, honoring it, and rewarding it: this is how we build young people who actually become adults who think for themselves and confidently assert who they are in the solution to problems. And if some of our adult aura of "having it all figured out" (which is not true anyway) has to be sacrificed at the altar of these moments, even better. This is about more than just interpersonal respect between students and teachers. This is about our own respect for our true responsibility: preparing these young people for a successful future.

FREE-FLOATING PRACTICAL ADVICE

I began this book with the idea that I would start with the 'big picture of you and why you teach, to hopefully inspire you to think first of the basic frame and structure from which the rest of your teaching strategy would be built. Call it mindset, dreams, big plans, philosophy– I moved from there further and further down the line through the more practical and concrete concerns of teaching.

Only in the latter third of this book did I get to the stuff that actually occurs *inside the classroom* on any given day. This was by design. I think so many of the challenges we face in the teaching profession are properly won and lost before we even set foot in the classroom, through mindset, authenticity, careful planning, and set routines and procedures. Only when that structure is in place and happening nearly 100 percent of the time will many of the classic day-to-day problems fade out and enable you to truly refine your classroom management craft.

There is still, however, plenty of hands-on teaching lore I've picked up over years of trial, failure, and observation of some truly badass educational professionals. They don't have an order or even necessarily direct connections to one another, so I will just open fire here and hope you find some of them to be applicable.

Be Present and Stay Mobile

Do you have a teacher desk? Minimize its use. Teacher desks are like bases on your campaign battle map. They're the places that station your daily essentials and provide a measure of stability for rest and refit.

Like on the battle map, however, they are not the places where the struggle is brought to a successful conclusion. The troops need to roll out of the base gate and go "outside the wire" to get anything meaningful done– to expend energy and put themselves in harm's way.

So it is for you. Your kids are teeming with youthful life. Their heads are full of their own concerns (many of which have nothing to do with education), their own social drama, and mild to active resentment at being shut up in a building all day. These problems are exacerbated by the great new phone technologies that provide a stealthy way of escape from whatever reasons there are to stay on task.

To win the battle for the territory of their minds requires far more than just an interesting subject and "work that needs to be done." We cannot remain in our bases. We must be out in the field, circulating at all times. Only here can we keep technology and social forces in check while being available for questions or clarifications. Only here can we monitor kids and get a good idea for who truly understands and who might be having trouble, but is too afraid or indifferent to express it. An added bonus is a much better understanding of your students as individuals and the little quirks they have that can help you build relationships. I can think of countless student relationships that were enriched for me by the small things I observed while circulating every day, from handwriting to kinds of doodling, to the kinds of questions on which individual students get stuck. The students appreciate this, because above all, remaining as omnipresent as we can in the classroom also sends a powerful and continuous message that we are active and care about the outcome of the lesson/unit/year, and that we are *here* at all times to help our kids.

When we are frequently seated at a desk, we send the opposite message in the most powerful way– nonverbally. Body language and presence counts for a lot. When we are slouched at a desk, absorbed in something, we make apparent that we are physically and mentally disconnected from our students as people, and whatever it is they need to understand and accomplish. Besides, teacher desks very often just become massive junkyards for clutter and other crap. I roll out of my seat after final preparations each morning, I get back into it for about 20 minutes at lunch, and during my plan period if I have grading or planning to do. Otherwise, I'm "outside the wire" all day, and I feel like that's where we belong, even when it's hard.

Use Words When Necessary

When I teach writing, I like to tell my students to pack as much meaning into as few words as possible. People can get caught up in trying to sound smart and use big words to impress, and I explain to my students that to an intelligent reader, these attempts bloat the writing, making it self-important and boring. Folks can read Shakespeare and get the wrong idea about why he used complex words. His metaphorical language often had two or three meanings present; when he used a big word, he chose it because that was the word with the exact meaning and complexity for what he needed. Conversely, if your brain is thinking "dog," and you insist on writing "canine companion," to any reader that's not a huge fan of alliteration, you don't sound smarter: you sound like an asshole.

The big word becomes necessary when truly capturing the meaning of what you are trying to say would take so many small words put together, that it's actually far more efficient and effective to use the one big word. For example, my eighth graders had trouble with 'flamboyant.' "Why not use some other, easier word? Who uses the word 'flamboyant?'" I would explain that for some people, especially in the entertainment industry, "tending to attract attention because of their exuberance, confidence, and stylishness" is a perfect description to use for a part of who they are. I could use something like that 20-syllable definition made up of simpler words, or I could use the 3-syllable 'flamboyant.' I take the opportunity to show the kids why higher-level vocabulary is important: it enables us to fill less breath with more substance.

I believe this general principle to be true in other ways: when teaching or explaining anything, the more meaning and substance you can pack into the least amount of words, the better. We get told all the time in professional development that the teacher should not be talking for the whole class. It's a great piece of advice because we all remember 'that teacher' we had in school that droned on endlessly until our brains melted. But it's not really about less teacher talk; it's about doing more with less, like having the routines in place that I mentioned earlier. The less you have to explain every day, the more space you have to get deeper with the talking you actually do, and the more space the kids have to explore that depth and ask questions.

Likewise for your classroom expectations. I view the use of my voice as a finite resource that loses effectiveness and engagement the more it is employed. I don't want to waste any of its use on reminding kids of what I expect. I try to communicate with them nonverbally whenever possible. This can be simple, like the constant classroom circulation. Physical proximity to students is a constant reminder of teacher expectations, so I try to not let any section of my classroom go too long without my physical presence passing through. It can also be complex, like being myself enough that the students come to understand the specific meanings of various kinds of body language or facial expressions, used for effect.

As the weeks go by, I can communicate more and more with less and less words. I stay utterly consistent in my verbal and nonverbal response to things that happen in class, so that an environment develops in which the students need no communication at all in response to anything they do because they already know what's coming. This allows my actual words to have the maximum power for when they are needed: helping guide my students to the next level in instruction.

Hard Power Is the Nuclear Option

Hopefully you've picked up by now that I favor building and maintaining high expectations, routines, procedures, and class culture to such an extent that students always know what to expect, what to do, and what the effects will be of any action they take. The less directions you give, the better. As I've mentioned, this is in part to keep students engaged: the more you are talking and the more you have to explain, the more boring and overbearing you will be. But the implications here are greater than just student engagement.

There is a strength in having such high expectations, routines, procedures, and culture that you rarely have to use your voice. I like to think of this as 'soft' power. It's like water, flowing over the students constantly and influencing their every physical and mental move in an almost imperceptible way. It is never brought to bear in an abrupt or direct fashion once it's in place. I hope you build up as much soft power as possible. Maintained, it will never dry up and will never inspire rebellion.

What I think of as 'hard' power, on the other hand, is the blunt force bomb, the direct verbal order. We draw from it when we are first setting expectations in place and then later when soft power doesn't have enough sway to keep them maintained. It is finite and potentially high-explosive, but it carries with it far more influence in the moment. It gives the student an either/or proposition: to follow the instruction, no matter how half-heartedly, or to engage in a public conflict with the teacher and willingly embrace the label of outlaw.

It's got a seductive power in the moment, and it's one I succumbed to far too often in my first few years as a teacher. To an extent, it even fit what the students would have expected from me: as a two hundred pound athlete with a shaved head, I get asked all the time if I was a wrestler or a Marine. My first day in class, every kid I have expects a drill sergeant personality, an intimidator.

When I struggled with classroom management, I wound up playing the part. It sucks. Yelling is verbal abuse, especially for the kids in the room that have nothing to do with whatever it is you're mad about. I've seen a few clandestine cell phone videos of some teachers losing their cool with students, and it's awful, but the worst part is knowing that if you had filmed some moments of my first few years, appearing "out of context," it would be just as bad. The context, however, isn't necessary. Yelling is a bad example, makes you look professionally unfit, and the kids in the room don't deserve it, period. When we have let stress, disappointment, and failure take us to the point of using brutish, ugly, or shouting intimidation methods to get students to comply with our demands, we have lost sight of what matters. This is supposed to be about the love of kids and the learning of important things.

Even the compliance we get from an angry order is a hollow one. We've gotten a behavior changed, not something learned. "Well, now the other kids can learn!" you might say, but the fact is many of them will be waiting for the next time somebody pushes your buttons enough to get you barking at the class again. It's tense and unpleasant. This is not an environment in which a culture of learning and engagement can be built. I remember speaking with my kids at the end of each of my first couple of years. We had done some good things together, but the one thing they repeated many times in their little goodbye talks and notes was "you got mad a lot." How sad is that? What teacher wants to be remembered in this fashion?

With each passing year, I raised my voice less and less, but it took me longer to realize the folly in using hard power at all. It should be kept in reserve, for emergencies only. The students should know it's there, of course: a bottom line beyond which they cannot go. Soft power however, should be the greatest influence on students; so much so that students will regulate their own behavior without commands, motivated by engagement, respect, or (hopefully) fear of looking like a jerk in front of their peers. I know that when I use hard power now, I always regard it as a failure. I reflect later and ask myself why the student(s) needed a direct order in that instant. Why did they not already clearly understand what was expected and how to do it? Why were they choosing to do something they shouldn't have, and why had I failed to anticipate the eventuality? What can I do next time to ensure that I don't have to resort to commands or public orders? How did this student not know exactly what the consequences of their actions would be, such that they might have been curious to 'test the waters?' I try to implement the fix as quickly as possible.

In a pinch, if I've *got* to use a direct command, I do it positively. Meaning, instead of telling a kid to *stop* doing something, I tell them to *begin* doing the thing they need to be doing. Negative commands ("stop talking!") have nothing to do with whatever it is the student is supposed to be learning, and are a perfect invitation to an argument that derails learning for everyone in the vicinity (student angrily denying/justifying the talking). When a student is talking over their blank sheet of paper, and for whatever reason I can't get over there to speak with the student one-on-one (always preferable), I can fire off a quick, deadpan "begin number one."

That's in a pinch, *if* I cannot speak one-on-one. Otherwise, I come to the student in question, and if I'm really doing my job, begin not with an accusation, or even a command, but a question! (e.g., "Why haven't you started?" or "Are you having some trouble with #1?") This does so many things that are so much better than saying "stop talking!" across the classroom. For one thing, I avoid the pointless negative command and the invitation to conflict. Many kids will be happy to take up that invitation when you have chosen to publicly call them out in front of their peers (who likes that?). For another thing, it keeps the communication focused on what needs to be achieved. Really, who cares about the behavior? Your ego cares because it's annoying, but that's a personal thing. Learning and achievement are the important things. And I've been surprised how many times I uncover a legitimate lack of understanding that is remediable with a little help from me– and how disarmed the student is when he or she realizes that I'm not coming over to get them in trouble, but to re-focus them on what I want them to understand.

Whatever you do, don't end up as that teacher who's got their voice raised, tense and barking directions or denouncing their class several times per week. It's like the coach yelling in the locker room of an 0-10 team; it's sad, pathetic, and creates a suffocating atmosphere of defeat that anyone in the vicinity can perceive. When hard power is used repeatedly, it is exhausted, and then there's nothing left. No respect, no culture, no credibility. Your class becomes just a room full of miserable people waiting for the next round of trouble. It's similar to a real use of the 'nuclear option'– the fallout is *bad*.

Make Your Classroom a Living Environment

Those walls in our classrooms: how should they be used? Sometimes we get told what to do with them, like chart progress, make a word wall, or display student work. That's all quite good, although it requires commitment. Any part of your classroom that is not consistently updated or used is going to become just a blur in the background, even to you. A word wall sitting there sadly blank in March (or with two words on it from October) is not just an eyesore; it's a glaring reminder of some way in which you're not achieving your goals. Your students will quickly forget to even look at it, but I believe it has a passively demoralizing effect.

It would be great if we could all consistently update the "active" parts of our classroom walls, and it's something I'm still trying to improve. If you're not already doing it, however, I would pick one thing you can commit to updating consistently throughout the year, and just do that to start. Then maybe add another thing next year. Make that one part of your class consistently alive and it will be for your students. They will begin to look for the updates, which is another layer of general engagement with your class. Good stuff!

I do not mean to say leave the rest blank. As best you can, make the rest an extension of your own unique brain and personality. Ditch the boilerplate mantras and teacher jokes on posters that you can buy in the teacher store in that strip mall. The kids have seen so many of those, their effect will literally be spent in the first twenty minutes of day one. Get a poster from a favorite film of yours instead, for example: something that means something to you. The kids will tune that out after day one as well, mostly, but if or when they don't, that's a *story*– and it's your story. Or if film doesn't work, something else: sports, music, cooking, travel, etc. Make your classroom unique to their experience.

Another added benefit to this is that occasionally *you* will look at it for the first time in a while and get reminded of something important about yourself– something that sets you apart in the teaching life. Every once in a while, when I'm stuck on something during a plan period or a summer day when I come in to do work, I stroll around my class, looking at my Walt Whitman and Kerouac framed quotes, my TS Eliot concept art, my road trip pictures, my reproduced painting from an underground East German literary journal, and I get reminded of how awesome my own learning journey has been. It always brings a good feeling: I did it *my* way. And I can do more.

CONCLUSION

I have no illusions that any of the observations I've made or techniques I've described here are new. An experienced person might well have hit something in this book and inwardly thought: *Ah, he got that from* _____. Perhaps I did! Or someone I came to trust and respect as an expert mentor taught it to me, and I was ignorant of the source that inspired them. Or maybe there are certain truths in human relationships that have seemed to show themselves in many different situations, and I happened to stumble across one in my own experience and write about it. To attempt to be truly original in the field of educating kids after thousands of years of human experience and civilization is a futile enterprise.

And why try? There are useful nuggets of wisdom in many different tried and tested schools of thought. After over twenty years of deeply studying the human experience in my adult life, I've made many connections and conclusions that have influenced my classroom– far more than could ever be covered in a single book. The important thing is to begin your study today– to improve, little by little, yourself and your practice. Along the way, follow the great mantra of Bruce Lee: "Absorb what is useful; Reject what is useless."

Lee founded a unique martial art, after all, called jeet kune do. His idea was to take pieces from all practical things he had absorbed in his life about combat (not limited to specific fighting skills) and apply them to actual combat, free from dogma or prejudice. In the end, he even rejected the idea of forming a school around his approach. It would have been too formal, codified, and prejudiced against the absorption of new and useful information. This is an excellent guiding principle (if often frustrating) for its lack of structure.

There are many, many books out there about how to teach effectively. Check them out, and don't just read the words; read the *authors* and their intentions, the reasons for the development of their strategies, and the classrooms in which they were tested. Rather than looking to any one of them as a Bible from which you should be able to draw *all* solutions, look at them as applied solutions to specific problems. Maybe they provide an answer to a problem you're having on your journey. Much depends on how well their strategies play to *your* strengths and minimize *your* weaknesses.

Find teachers, guides, and mentors that are aware of your strengths and weaknesses, and listen to them. They have a uniquely useful insight into *you* that is difficult to diagnose on your own and impossible to find in a book. This insight will be invaluable in moving you along your path faster and more efficiently. Even then it will still be a long time before you master the art. Teaching is a game of years. Speaking personally, I'm skeptical of the idea that someone can come out of college or alternate teaching programs totally prepared for success. Even student teaching is not the same as having *your* classroom with *your* kids, all year long. Preparatory training is the *beginning* of your quest.

Rome, as we've all heard, was not built in a day. The Romans themselves offer a pretty illustrative example: during the centuries of their ascendancy they were famous for suffering disastrous defeats followed by a reflective and humble process. They never allowed defeat to cause them to doubt their own importance or to consider surrender. They sought rather to learn and acquire the best practices of their opponents while reforming their own institutions to better prevent future defeats. No traditional approach was too sacred for the Romans as they bounced back stronger time and again. Yet underneath their process of change remained the bedrock of their belief in the supremacy of what they brought to the world.

The Romans absorbed, elevated, and exported literacy, engineering, law, architecture and many other invaluable avenues of knowledge. They invented little, but through a combination of extreme confidence and learning humility, taught the world much. Discipline and flexibility were introduced as paired doctrinal principles by the Roman Army, and it showed in their record of ultimate success and the legacy they left. So let it be for you in your journey to teach– and to learn.

This is not just a craft or even a noble profession, although it is both of those things. It is, above all, an opportunity to leave a real legacy, improving the world one classroom and one person at a time. In case you haven't looked around any time recently, civilization could use the help. I ask you to invest in that process in the long-term, establish that legacy, and see where it takes you. The rewards are priceless. The greatest known swordsman and martial arts teacher/writer in Japanese history, Miyamoto Musashi, ended his life as a contented hermit in a mountain hut– and a legend. He wasn't wealthy, but his constant drive for improvement in life's arts and the example of his teaching cast a shadow that loomed for centuries.

And so might yours. After the massive dollars are spent on education, the plans are made for district curriculum, the buildings are administered and organized by school leaders, and the students are enrolled, there you will be at the fine point where learning happens. Don't ever forget that YOU are the EDGE of teaching.